Dianna,
Thanks you

Paulette

NEVER
AT
EASE

Memoir of a Mountie

Paulette Breau

 FriesenPress

Suite 300 - 990 Fort St
Victoria, BC, V8V 3K2
Canada

www.friesenpress.com

Copyright © 2019 by Paulette Breau
First Edition — 2019

Edited by Sean Hazelton

All rights reserved.

No part of this publication may be reproduced in any form, or by any means, electronic or mechanical, including photocopying, recording, or any information browsing, storage, or retrieval system, without permission in writing from FriesenPress.

ISBN
978-1-5255-5758-3 (Hardcover)
978-1-5255-5759-0 (Paperback)
978-1-5255-5760-6 (eBook)

1. BIOGRAPHY & AUTOBIOGRAPHY, LAW ENFORCEMENT

Distributed to the trade by The Ingram Book Company

Chapter One

🍁

IT WAS A DULL, GREY autumn day as I stepped onto the Via train in Brantford. I was headed to Toronto to testify as a claimant in the Merlo Davidson class action lawsuit. The lawsuit alleged gender and/or sexual orientation-based discrimination, bullying and harassment against female RCMP[1] members and public service employees. It was my turn to be interviewed by the retired judge appointed to hear the claims.

I was advised that I could bring a friend along for moral support and I really needed one. I was relieved to see that my friend, Jennifer, was already on the train so I sat down beside her. Ironically, I was sitting in a seat facing the back of the train. Like I was going back in time. To the beginning.

In fact, I had been living in the past for well over a year as I prepared my claim. Although Jennifer was talking to me, my mind was elsewhere. I was nervous. I was about to meet a complete stranger and tell him my deepest, darkest secrets.

Could I trust him? Would he doubt me? Would he believe me? My story is almost unbelievable, but I actually lived it and it was real.

BY the time we arrived at Union Station, my mind was a blur, so I was just following Jennifer. I was focused on what lay ahead. I kept telling

---

1   Royal Canadian Mounted Police, also known as Mounties

myself, "Just keep following her. Don't panic, don't cry. Breathe". It was getting closer to the time of my interview—the time I would finally get to tell my story. I was feeling anxious and emotional, struggling to hold back the tears.

When I arrived at the building, Jennifer asked for directions while I continued to follow her in a daze, thankful that she was taking charge. As the elevator went up and the doors opened, we were greeted by a woman we hadn't met before. She introduced herself as the Executive Director of the Office of the Independent Assessor in the settlement of the Merlo Davidson Class Action. I advised her that Jennifer was also a claimant and asked whether that would cause any issues if she sat in on my interview. The woman said she would ask the judge and then walked us down a hallway.

Another woman passed us who looked teary eyed. We both looked at each other and I said, "I think that she is a claimant too". Jennifer agreed.

We waited outside the judge's office as the woman went in. The office windows overlooked the rainy skies of Toronto. Then she came back out and said the judge had no issues with Jennifer sitting in on the interview, but reminded her that she could not talk during the interview.

Telling us to come in, we sat at a round table and she introduced me to another woman in the room who was the lawyer assigned to review my submission. And then she introduced us to the judge. I recognized him from the picture and video I had watched on the class action website. The judge was a small man and very soft-spoken.

They asked my permission to audio and video tape the interview. The audio was a backup for the videotape and would be destroyed at the end of the process. The video would be used by them when reviewing the interview, in case they needed to listen to any details again. I gave my consent.

The judge had a stack of papers in front of him that appeared to be a copy of my submission. The lawyers told me that they would be taking notes during the interview. The judge said that this was more like a conversation than an interview. He thanked me for coming forward and asked me why I'd wanted to become an RCMP officer.

As I looked past him through the windows, looking at the grey skies, I began my story.

Chapter Two

🍁

SAINT JOHN, NEW BRUNSWICK IS the oldest incorporated city in Canada. My parents met in that city when they both worked at St. Joseph's Hospital. I was born in Saint John and it's the place I still call "home".

My father was a respiratory technician at the hospital and my mother also worked there in housekeeping until she had her first child, then she was a stay-at-home mom. Eventually, my parents had four children and we lived in a geared-to-income townhouse with three bedrooms, one bathroom, and small backyard. The three girls shared one bedroom, my brother and parents the other two.

My father continued to work at the hospital and became the president of the CUPE² local. He travelled a lot, leaving my mother to look after four young kids on her own. We were not well-off and most of our clothes were hand-me-downs, but we didn't really care. We had food, shelter and beds to sleep in so didn't really consider ourselves to be poor, although others might have thought so.

I was a tomboy and loved playing with the boys—boot camp, GI Joe, going for adventures in the woods. I never wanted a Barbie doll, just a Jim Cobra, a cowboy doll with a gun and a horse. I always loved sports and

---

2   Canadian Union of Public Employees

played every sport I could, including basketball and soccer. I tried out for every team possible at school and made every single one of them except volleyball. When I got older, I played fastball. Watching sports was also important to me—I was a huge football and hockey fan. I was a fan of Peter Dellarivera, receiver for the Montreal Alouettes, and Guy LaFleur of the Montreal Canadiens.

*

OUR family had two things we shared in common: one was the love of animals and the other was a love of music. We always had a dog or cats, and the radio was always on.

I was not unhappy, but as a kid I already knew I wanted something more. I made my mom a promise: I promised that I would have a career, own a sports car, own a house, get married and have kids. I wanted to be independent and not have to rely on anyone else to survive. I was smart in school and motivated. I was already planning what my life would be like.

Our neighbor used to read True Detective magazines and when he was finished with them, he gave them to me. Reading about how detectives solved crimes, usually murders, was fascinating to me and I wanted to have an exciting job like that.

Chapter Three

🍁

GROWING UP IN SAINT JOHN, it seemed as if there was an abundance of crime all around me, and I was fascinated by it from an early age. When I was young, I honestly believed that there were dead bodies everywhere.

At the age of nine or ten years, I remember seeing police cars with their lights on, parked across the street. The lights were reflecting off the windows of our apartment. It was so exciting!

Apparently, a five-year-old boy was missing and the police and neighbours were searching for him. Earlier in the afternoon, that boy had been playing in the woods, along with a bunch of kids, including my younger sister. He was at the back of the group and no one noticed he had gone missing.

I could hear the voices of the searchers as they called out for him. It was dark. I could see their flashlights scanning across the street.

In the end, we heard the sad news that the body of the missing boy had been found, hidden in a concrete culvert. His throat had been slit open and his body covered in bite marks. During the search, it was revealed that a family relative confessed he was playing a game with the boy and had accidentally hung him with a rope. Then he'd unintentionally cut his throat while trying to cut the rope. He claimed he'd panicked and tried to make it look like an animal had attacked him and hidden the body. The police took him away. Shortly after, the family moved away.

SOMETIME after this, a pregnant woman was killed at the back of our school. She had been dragged behind a car, leaving blood and skin spread all over the school grounds. He then cut her open and removed the fetus because her boyfriend didn't think the baby was his. He left her body on the front steps of the school, her skin and blood over the soccer field and the front steps. Our classes were cancelled so that the police could clean up the crime scene.

LATER still, a body was found behind our babysitter's apartment. Some kids had been playing in the freshly fallen snow and kicked a mound of snow, exposing a human head. After the police had left the scene, our family drove over to see where the body had been found. The smell of rotting flesh is unforgettable. You could still see a layer of human skin in the dirt.

THEN came the Noah Winters case in 1974. The first news report stated that a human body part had been found at the dump. A scavenger, looking for stuff at the dump, had ripped open a garbage bag, exposing a body part. It turned out there were three body parts in that bag—three human legs.

The police searched the city dump looking for more body parts, and found the remains of two people, a man and a woman. Noah Winters, identified as the prime suspect, was arrested. Near the back of his house the police discovered two more bodies buried in a shallow grave. They were identified as his neighbours—a father and a son.

Amazingly, several years later, I would actually meet the forensics RCMP officer who had worked the Winters case. He pulled out the photos of the case and told me about it. It was as fascinating as I had remembered—bodies buried in the mud!

Investigators had to boil the meat off the bones to determine which leg belonged to which body since there was no DNA back then. He explained, as he showed me the crime scene photos, that although the Winters' house had been repainted and bloody carpets cleaned, enough blood remained for the police to be able to link him to the bodies.

INCREDIBLY, there was still more violence in our community. On December 25, 1974, the murder of two Moncton police officers rocked the province. I remember hearing how the victims were made to dig their own graves before being shot in the head. They were buried in those dark, cold shallow graves. Their murderers were convicted and became the last two people to be given the death penalty in Canada.

EVEN in school, there were episodes of violence. One day in biology class, the teacher caught me passing a note to my friend. She made me move my desk to the very front of the class, right beside hers. I was so embarrassed. I had never done anything like that before.

As it turned out, my friend was a bad influence. She was into drugs and boys. One day her boyfriend pointed a gun at me because he thought I was trying to get his girlfriend to break up with him. In fact, I was—I thought she deserved better than that.

ALL this is to say that I was exposed to an unusual amount of crime and violence in my early years and I was fascinated by every bit of it.

Chapter Four

✤

IN THE SUMMER OF 1979, our family went to visit our relatives in northern New Brunswick. While we were there, my grandfather asked my father to move back since he had terminal cancer and needed someone to care for him. I remember voting as a family and it was tied: three to stay and three to move. My father made lots of promises to each of us. If I agreed to move, I would get a bird—I'm still waiting for that bird!

So it was decided, we would be moving. Within a week our family was packed up and we'd moved to Neguac, four hours away from everything I knew. I didn't even have a chance to say good-bye to my friends.

In my dreams about my future, I had seen myself living at home and going to the University of New Brunswick in Saint John. We were poor and I knew going to university would be expensive, but when we moved away, I didn't know how I would ever afford to go to school to continue my education.

ALTHOUGH my parents were French-speaking, we were brought up English-speaking, as there were no bilingual schools in Saint John. The only time I heard my parents speak French was when they were fighting because they thought we wouldn't know what they were fighting about. Neguac, on the other hand, was a French-speaking community and very different from Saint John. Nonetheless, violence seemed to follow me wherever I went.

*

ONE of the first friends I made was a fellow named Kenneth Esson. He was a foster child who lived just down the street from us. He spoke English and was around the same age as I was.

Kenneth and I hung out together at our house a lot. He was a very polite and shy fellow who loved to play his guitar and sing. I would sing along with him and he'd teach me how to play the guitar. Kenneth wanted to start a band, saying I could sing with him. What kid doesn't want to sing in a band?

He spoke French and went to the local high school in Neguac, but I didn't speak French so I went to the English high school at Miramichi Valley High, about an hour away. In time, I made more friends as I played sports and, as time went on, I saw less and less of Kenneth.

YEARS later, I learned that on August 14, 1986, someone had sexually assaulted, and then stabbed two girls near Neguac. The thirteen-year-old girl had died and the other victim, fourteen years old, survived her wounds because the family dog had lain on her, which had stopped the bleeding. The surviving victim gave a description of her attacker, which appeared on the front page of the newspaper. It looked just like my friend, Kenneth Esson!

Shortly after the newspaper had printed the sketch, Kenneth changed his hair from straight to curly and grew a moustache. No one thought anything about it. Three weeks later, a nineteen-year-old girl from Neguac was found dead in the gravel pit right behind her parents' house, only a mile from our own house. A month and a half later the RCMP arrested and charged Kenneth Esson with two counts of first degree murder and one count of attempted murder.

A couple of years later, when I was home on holidays, I did a ride along with the local RCMP. While at the detachment, an RCMP officer pulled out the Kenneth Esson file and showed it to me. Contained in the file were the crime scene photos. I knew the victim, but could not recognize her. I was in disbelief at how brutal her death had been and how close I had once again been to violence and death.

Chapter Five

♦

IN NEGUAC, THE RCMP ARE the local police. My father became an auxiliary member and my mother a jail guard for the RCMP. As a result, I came to know all the members of this particular RCMP detachment. The members would stop by my parents' home for coffee and share their stories about policing. What an exciting job! That is when I knew I wanted to be an RCMP officer.

LATER that year, at the local fair in Chatham, I saw a police recruitment display. I approached the officer working at the booth and told him I wanted to become a police officer. He broke my heart when he told me I was too small, too short. The minimum height was 5'4". I was 5'3".

He told me to keep playing sports and stay in school and maybe someday those rules might change. I did just that! I continued to play sports, obtained good marks in school and learned to speak French.

AFTER graduating from high school in 1981, I got a job working at a bookstore in Bathurst, an hour north from where my parents lived. My sister and I moved into an apartment and worked together in the store where I ended up becoming the manager.

Money was tight as minimum wage was only $5.00 an hour, so I moved into a rooming house. Then in 1983, my boss approached me about taking over a new store in Douglastown. It was thirty minutes from my parents' house and they agreed to let me move back home.

*

ONE day in August, an RCMP cruiser was parked in front of our house, blocking the highway and detouring the traffic, as there was a parade in town. The officer, whom I knew, was standing outside his cruiser redirecting traffic.

It was a very hot day, so I brought him out a glass and a pitcher of water and asked if I could look inside his cruiser. I jokingly told him I might only ever get to sit in *the back* of a cruiser and he asked me why. When I told him I could never become a police officer because I was too short, he told me that rule no longer applied. I was surprised, but very excited when he told me I should apply.

A few days later, I approached the sergeant in charge of the detachment, Steve, and asked him what I needed to do to apply. He told me the first step was to write the RCMP entrance exam, which was held right there at the detachment. I didn't want to tell anyone I was applying until I knew I would be accepted, so I asked him not to tell my parents.

WHEN the date for me to write the exam arrived, I nervously entered the detachment and met with the sergeant. He brought me to an interview room, handed me the exam and told me to complete only the sample questions. He placed an X on the page and told me not to go any further until he said so.

When he left the room, I read the instructions and completed the sample questions, then waited for him to return. I waited and waited and waited. At one point, since I was in an interview room, I wondered if maybe he was watching me behind two-way glass, checking to see if I would follow his instructions.

Eventually, I could hear footsteps outside the door and spoke out, "Excuse me," trying to get that person's attention.

When the door finally opened, the secretary appeared in the doorway asking, "Are you all done?"

"Done?" I stammered, "I'm still waiting to start!"

It turns out, Steve had been called away from the detachment on another matter and had forgotten about me waiting in the interview room. The secretary called him and asked him to come back to the office.

A few minutes later, Steve appeared in front of me, red-faced and apologetic. "Are you expected home for supper?" When I replied that I was, he said, "You'd better call and tell your mom you're going to be late!" I did, and came clean to her about where I was and what I was doing.

After sitting and waiting there for two hours, I was at last able to start the exam. Obviously, I'd already proven myself as being good at following orders. I jokingly told people years later that I was famous for the taking the greatest length of time to write the RCMP entrance exam.

A few weeks later, I was thrilled to be told that I had passed the entrance exam and I received the application forms, which I quickly completed and sent back to the recruiting office. Following that, I learned that the RCMP would complete a background investigation on me and the next steps would be an interview, followed by medical and physical examinations.

It was a few months before I was called to Bathurst for my interview. I was excited because, if I passed the interview, then I would only have the medical and physical tests to complete.

On the day of the interview, I drove to the Bathurst Detachment.

Arriving, I signed in and waited in the lobby.

There was another person waiting to be interviewed as well. He went in first. Then about an hour later he emerged and I was called to come in. The recruiter was a French-speaking member and he conducted the interview in French. After the interview was completed, the recruiting officer asked me to wait outside in the lobby. This was it! I would soon know what my future was going to look like, one way or the other.

The recruiter called me back into the room and congratulated me. I had passed the interview! He told me that there was a female troop coming up in less than three months and, if I passed the medical and physical test, I would be going to Depot[3]. My dream of joining the RCMP was only months away from coming true!

Then the recruiter asked me why I hadn't gone to school in Neguac. I told him I was brought up English and learned to speak French when I'd moved to Neguac. That seemed to cause a hesitation in his attitude. He told me that I would have to take a French test to see if I could go to Depot in a French troop, and arranged for me to take the test as soon as possible. The date was set for January 28, 1986, and the test would take place in Moncton.

My father agreed to drive me to Moncton as I'd never driven there before. We drove down the morning of the test. Since it was a two-hour drive, we left at 5:00 am. As luck would have it, that morning we had a torrential downpour. At some point, my car stalled due to the large amount of water sitting on top the roads. That really added tension to what was already a very stressful drive. Thankfully, we arrived just minutes before the 8:00 am start time. The exam took about an hour to write.

When I met up with my father after the test, I'll never forget the first thing he said to me: "Paulette, the space shuttle blew up."

---

3   RCMP Academy, Depot Division in Regina, Saskatchewan

At first, his words didn't register in my brain so I asked him to repeat it. He said the space shuttle had been launched and then exploded. I remember how we walked across the street to a store that had TVs in the window. There we were standing on a street in Moncton, watching in horror as the space shuttle *Challenger* blew up killing all seven crew members including a school teacher. I would never forget the date that I wrote my French test.

A few days later, I received the bad news—I had failed my French test! I wouldn't be going to Depot with the French troop, but could still continue the recruitment process to be part of an English troop. The medical and physical exams came next.

I received a booklet to help me prepare for the physical test. It contained exercises that I should do to be prepared. One exercise showed a man doing female push-ups. When I tried to do one, I thought I must be doing it wrong. So I looked over the pictures in the booklet and tried again. I couldn't figure out how to do them.

I asked my brother to come in and watch me do one. He agreed that they looked difficult and showed me how to do a male push-up. It was so much easier to do than the push-ups in the booklet.

At that time, the fitness standard for women was nine female push-ups and thirty sit-ups in a minute, as well a stress test. I started with female push-ups. It wasn't easy, but I wanted this badly and I was going to do it so I kept working at it.

Once I got strong enough to do female push-ups, I decided to challenge myself by doing the male version. I would go for a jog and after my run, I would do my sit-ups and push-ups.

Eventually, a date was set to complete my medical and physical tests. Once again, I was excited about this news since this meant I was near the end of the process and would be ready to be hired. I was sent to see a doctor at the military base in Gagetown. After the medical exam, I completed the fitness test. I did twenty-five male push-ups! The recruiting officer was very impressed!

I received a letter advising me that I was a successful applicant and that I would be placed on the national waiting list to be hired. I had passed, and now it became a waiting game.

IN the meantime, I continued to babysit for RCMP members in my spare time, and hung out at the detachment where members would show me training videos that would help me get ready for my career in policing. Whenever I was out jogging and a cruiser would pass me on the road, they would activate their lights and sirens to cheer me on. This reinforced my desire to join the RCMP and made me feel as if I were already a part of their community. I continued to run and work out and called the recruiting office in Fredericton every week. I figured that one day, if I kept calling, my file would be at the top of the pile when they needed to hire someone.

Chapter Six

🍁

IN OUR SMALL CORNER OF the world, the summer of 1986 was one filled with violence, murder and fear. First, Alain Legere and two other men were arrested for the murder of a shopkeeper and the attempted murder of his wife—it was the talk of the Miramichi.

Later that summer, there was the attack on two young girls that left one dead and the other near death, as well as the murder of a young woman in Neguac by Kenneth Esson.

For the first time, people were locking their doors and were afraid to let their children out of their sight. In fact, I met a Mountie who'd recently graduated and he couldn't believe how violent New Brunswick was. For a small province, it seemed to have more than its fair share of violent crimes.

WHILE I was waiting to get hired, I'd purchased a book about the RCMP and read the amazing stories about their proud history. It was so exciting to learn how the infamous Sam Steele rode west to fight the whiskey trade and then patrolled during the gold rush of the 1890s when thousands of prospectors journeyed to the remote Yukon.

I read about the "Lost Patrol", a group of Mounties that had set out from Fort McPherson, Northwest Territories on December 21, 1910, and were headed for Dawson, Yukon Territory, a trek of roughly 800 kilometers[4]. When they got lost, the patrol turned back toward Fort McPherson in a desperate race against cold and starvation. The grisly discoveries of the bodies of Taylor and Kinney, then Carter and Fitzgerald, were all made within 50 km of Fort McPherson between March 21 to 22, 1911.

I continued to be fascinated by Canadian crimes, including the story of the mad trapper who eluded the RCMP on foot for over a month and 240 km until he was shot and killed on the Eagle River in the Yukon. The book also talked about the modern-day Mounties who now included female officers. And *this* just made me want to be a Mountie more than ever.

AFTER a year, my medical and physical tests had expired, so I had to complete them again to remain active on the waiting list. To do this, I had to go to the RCMP headquarters in Fredericton. I'll never forget when the nurse was taking my blood pressure and a funny look came over her face. I asked her what was wrong and she said," You don't have a blood pressure!"

I joked, "That would make me dead".

She tried it again, same results. I would be the first dead person ever hired by the RCMP!

ABOUT a year and a half after I'd started the process, on January 13, 1987, I received a call from the RCMP recruiting officer, telling me that a position had become available and that I would be hired.

I said, "Yes!" as fast as I could.

Then the recruiting officer said, "But".

"But what?"

He said someone had backed out and that I'd have to be in Fredericton on Friday to be sworn in and fly to Regina on Saturday! I told him that

---

4   Approximately 500 miles

wouldn't be a problem—I'd waited a long time to get that call. After I hung up the phone, I suddenly became nervous. I was leaving for Regina on Saturday and there was a lot to do, including hiring someone to replace me at work. I quickly chose someone from the applications we had on file and said my goodbyes to all the people I knew in the mall before I left. It was the happiest and the scariest day of my twenty-three-year-old life!

MY parents drove me to Fredericton on the Thursday night. Very close friends of the family met us in Fredericton on Friday morning and we had breakfast together. Then, on on January 16, 1987, we drove to the RCMP Headquarters and I was sworn in. I swore allegiance to my country and the Queen, took an oath of secrecy, and also took a pledge that I was willing to serve anywhere in Canada. Little did I know how true that would become!

I was issued badge number 39286. At the time, I didn't know what that meant, but later I was told that the RCMP doesn't reuse its badges. This meant that I was the thirty-nine thousand two hundred and eighty-sixth RCMP officer hired. From 1873 to 1987, there had been 39,285 other officers hired as RCMP officers before me. I was no longer Paulette Breau, I was 39286.

ON Saturday morning, my parents drove me to the airport. It was the first time in my life that I would fly. As I walked up the stairs to the plane, I turned around and waved goodbye to my parents, then I boarded and flew out to Regina, Saskatchewan. Since I'd never flown before, I had no idea that my ears would be as sore as they were—it took days before my ears would pop and clear up!

Chapter Seven

❦

I TOOK A TAXI FROM the airport to Depot. We stopped to check in at the guardroom and then I was escorted to our dorm. As I walked through the doors of my new home, I saw thirty-two single beds lined up, sixteen on each side of the room, with two beds pushed together. After someone told me where my bed was located, I walked down the dorm, greeting and shaking hands with every person I met.

My new living area was called a "pit" and I had a pit partner. Together, we were responsible for keeping our pit clean. We each had three drawers and a small closet. It turned out the drawers were just large enough to put our uniforms in and there was no place for personal stuff. Later, we would be told to purchase a trunk to hold our personal belongings.

Then came another big surprise—there was only one room to shower in! It was a huge room with eight showerheads, and we would all have to shower together. The only thing we could do in private was use the toilet. As I recall, there were about ten sinks, seven washroom stalls and only one bathtub. We had to sleep together in one large dorm, shower together, change clothes together and eat together. I was glad no one had told me about this before I joined.

That first week, we were also fitted for our uniforms and had our pictures taken. It was unnerving to be told that one of the pictures was put on file to be used as our funeral picture, to be released by the RCMP if we were to die on duty.

WE were Troop 18 of fiscal year 86/87 but by the end of our training we would become a family. I'd volunteered to be the Admin Marker for our troop. The Right Marker was the person in charge of the troop. As Admin Marker, I was the second in charge. From the start, we were only called by our last names.

At 5:00 every morning we would wake up and get ready for morning inspections that took place in the drill hall at 6:30. Before we attended the drill hall, we had to clean our dorm, scrub the washrooms, and iron our wool blankets and pillows so that there were no wrinkles. Eventually, I got another pillow that I kept in my trunk. I would sleep on that one so that I didn't have to iron the other one. Anything to save time since there was so little of it to spare.

Everything had to look the same. The blankets on our beds all had to be folded the same way so we measured and marked our bedposts with black marker. And when you looked from one end of the dorm to the other, everything had to look identical and line up perfectly. We spent a lot of time eliminating even the smallest piece of lint or dust—any remaining lint or dust meant we were disciplined with push-ups, lots and lots of push-ups. Everything was supposed to be perfect, but of course it never was.

Many times during our six months in Depot, we would come back to our dorm to find that it had been trashed, meaning an instructor had come into our dorm and found there was something that didn't meet the standards they had set. Something as small as a single uniform button left undone meant that we had to put our dorm back together again before the next class started.

EVERY morning we attended the drill hall for lengthy inspections. At that time, morning drill took place before breakfast. One morning, the drill sergeant pulled on the back of my hair stating it was touching my collar. I thought I'd gotten my hair cut short enough, but apparently it wasn't. So it was back to the hairdresser to have it shortened even more.

ANOTHER morning, only two weeks into Depot, I fainted and fell face-first on the floor during drill inspection. We'd arrived early in the drill hall wearing our winter jackets and fur hats, making it very hot plus we hadn't yet had anything to eat. In fact, when I'd fainted, I just missed hitting the drill sergeant.

The first thing I remember when I came around was him yelling at me because I was bleeding on his drill floor. I'd cracked my front teeth and split my lip open.

This just gave my Drill Corporal something to tease me about. He would say, "Breau, nice lip!" and as my lip was healing, he would say "BREAU, your looks are improving!"

One day, I was the Right Marker of our troop, so I was in charge that day. The same Drill Corporal marched up to me and came to attention about two inches from my face.

He asked me," Breau what do you see?"

"A nice shiny button, Corporal!" I replied because all I could see was the button on his serge!

AFTER morning inspection, breakfast, and returning to our dorm to make sure we hadn't missed anything, we got ready for classes, all before 8:00 am. Our classes went from 8:00 am to noon. Then, when we finished classes at noon, we'd regroup and march to the lunch hall.

Lunchtime was an hour long, but we were required to sign up for a duty to be done over the lunch hour. Our group had to have a certain number of members in the band, choir and other activities. I'd signed up for choir, which started at 12:15 pm, three days a week, requiring me to eat my lunch within eight to ten minutes in order to make choir practices. Classes resumed at 1:00 pm and went until 4:30 pm.

FOR the first week or two in Depot, I'd been enjoying the food. But that changed quickly since they served the same food over and over again. Back then, there wasn't a salad bar or any other options so we could only eat what was served. Breakfast and lunch had to be eaten quickly as other duties as well as and cleaning the dorm needed to be done before classes. The only meal where we had time to sit and eat was supper, but the habit of eating my meals quickly has stayed with me to this day.

The food situation improved greatly when I found out there was a toaster at the back of the mess hall. The cafeteria always served cold unbuttered toast so, when I could make my own, it was such a simple pleasure to eat a warm buttered piece of toast. It was like being at home! Others must have felt the same way about the food because at that time the troops were ordering an average of $10,000 a month worth of take-out food to be delivered. We were always hungry!

THE Mess was like everything else in Depot—it was organized by rank and seniority. The senior troop sat at the only table with a tablecloth. When you arrived, you were the junior troop and would sit at the first table in the mess hall. As senior troops graduated, each troop would move up, not only in seniority but also in being one table closer to that linen tablecloth.

The senior troop's number is displayed in the Drill Hall, and when the senior troop graduates, the next troop in line is invited to attend their graduation ceremony to do the changing of the numbers. Taking the graduating troop's number down and putting up the new senior troop's number was a part of Depot's tradition. Every troop looked forward to the next troop's arrival so that they wouldn't be the junior troop anymore. Seniority meant everything.

LAW, driving, shooting, self-defence, swimming, physical fitness, first aid, CPR, note-taking, spit-shining our shoes, boots and Sam Brown[5], marching, jogging. And more push-ups. These were some of the skills we were learning every day.

One day, three other troop mates and I were called out of class. My first thought was, *Uh oh! Are we in trouble?* But then the instructor told us that we were going to be hiding weapons and drugs on our bodies and the rest of the troop members were going to search us and see if they could find the items we'd hidden.

The instructor gave me a plastic bag full of white powder. He told me to put it in my underwear and, if someone found it, to tell them I was on my menstrual period, and to wait and see if they would confirm it. The second item was a throwing star he told me to hide in my bra.

After we'd hidden the items, we were told to go back into the class and not mention anything. Then he told the rest of the troop that we were going to practise doing a proper search, and that the four of us might or might not have items hidden on our bodies.

One of my troop mates felt the bag I'd stuffed in my underwear and whispered in my ear, "Paulette are you on your period?" I whispered back that I was, but she didn't check to confirm it.

At the end of the exercise, we were told to leave the room and remove any items that had not been found during the search. I returned with the bag of white powder and the throwing star.

---

5   Gun belt

The instructor asked us one by one to tell the class what we each had and where we'd hidden it. I held out the bag of white powder and told the class that the person who'd searched me had found it, but believed me when I'd said I was on my period and didn't search that area any further. I also held out the throwing star that had been hidden in my bra. This would be a very important lesson.

Nobody likes to search other people, let alone their private areas. And people will lie to you. They don't want to get arrested. When an officer is searching a person's private area and they start to make a fuss, some people will stop searching, afraid of getting in trouble or being accused of inappropriate touching. I decided I would rather face a complaint than lose my life because someone had a gun hidden down his or her pants.

THEY were training us to become police officers and I loved almost every single minute of it, except typing. In New Brunswick, I'd never seen a typewriter in school let alone heard of a typing class. In Depot, we had to type 18 words per minute.

After our second typing class, I was the only person out of thirty-two who couldn't do this. But we had a total of fourteen one-hour classes and it took me those full fourteen hours to achieve 18 words per minute. Imagine my humiliation if I'd failed the police academy because I couldn't type!

WE each had to maintain a police notebook, and write something in our notebooks every single day, even if it was a day off. It was a challenge finding something every day to write in the dead of winter at Depot, but easy when we were out driving because there were a lot of suspicious jackrabbits at Depot—that was about all you would see while driving on a cold, dark night—and we could write about that.

FROM the moment I'd wanted to be a police officer and through the whole process of hiring, it had never experienced any issues. I was accepted by the members in my hometown and the recruiting process had been good, long but good. In training, during a physical fitness class, that our instructors told us the only reason we (females) were here at Depot was because the RCMP needed to improve their quota on the number of female members.

I knew that the first female recruits were hired in 1974, and so I assumed that females were not only needed but also wanted. I would soon find out that this was not always the case.

Chapter Eight

✦

AFTER ABOUT THREE MONTHS IN Depot, we had a long weekend for Easter. I decided to fly home for the four-day weekend. When I arrived, I found out my parents had planned a get together at their home. Along with family and friends, the local RCMP officers and their wives came over too!

I felt a real sense of belonging to the RCMP family I had in Neguac, and was growing attached to the RCMP family I had in Depot too. Although I still found it hard to believe that my dream of becoming a Mountie had come true, I knew I'd made the right career decision. I felt like the luckiest person in the world!

BACK again at Depot for more training, I was required to make a presentation. The topic was the death penalty. I spoke about the two Moncton Police officers who had been murdered on Christmas day, whose murderers were the last two people to be given the death penalty in Canada. And I spoke about my friend, Kenneth Esson.

How could I have been friends with someone who was on his way to becoming a serial killer? How could I not know? How would I feel if Kenneth had been given a death sentence?

I wanted to share with my troop mates that crimes as serious as murder can hit close to home, and that the death penalty had consequences beyond the person being executed.

DRIVING was also a big part of our training. We were expected to practice our driving at night and during weekends. My driving partner was from Montreal and was used to city driving, but I'd learned to drive in Neguac with no stoplights and only one stop sign in the whole village. We did our driving mostly on back roads and highways, not downtown streets.

One day, though, we were driving and there was a light flashing up ahead. I was about to drive past the flashing lights when the instructor slammed on the brakes. Turns out, it was a school crossing light. Well, we sure didn't have any of those in Neguac.

Another night, I was driving when my driving partner panicked because I'd turned left into oncoming traffic. I ended up driving over the median and back into the right lane of traffic. It wasn't the last time I would scare her!

ONE part of training I really didn't like was being exposed to tear gas. It was awful! Tear gas was one of the tools commonly used by the RCMP and, therefore, we were exposed to it so that if we ever encountered it during a call, we would be able to work our way through the discomfort and still react to any threats and continue to be of service. For this, we were enclosed in an airtight room and given a gas mask. When your name was called, you removed your mask and answered the question the instructor asked. We were told, if you dropped your mask, you'd have to go back into the room and do it over again.

Waiting for my name to be called, I thought the instructor had called my name, but it was actually another troop mate's name. So there I was, standing there with my gas mask in my hand choking. The instructor wasn't talking to me. I dropped my mask and ran out of the room. When I had to go back into the room, luckily, the gas had cleared by that point and I was able to retrieve my mask.

Although we practised with a gas mask, we weren't issued gas masks for at least another twenty years. Pepper spray, batons and tasers didn't exist in 1987. When I graduated from the police academy all I had was a gun. It would take years before I was issued any other use-of-force options.

AT that time, women RCMP officers wore different red serge uniforms than men. The men wore the traditional red tunic, riding pants, boots and Stetson hats. The women wore a V-neck tunic, blue skirt, black shoes and a pillbox hat. They were also issued a purse to carry the gun in—a purse! With a place to put my bullets in too! It was to be worn with my Red Serge. As soon as I could, I threw it out. I refused to carry that purse.

A few weeks before we graduated, the Musical Ride came to Depot. There, for the first time, I saw a woman wearing the men's uniform. She looked amazing sitting up there on her black horse. The sight inspired me, and I hoped that one day I could look like that. Little did I know that the female officer I saw would suffer from a terrible case of sexual harassment in her role as part of the Musical Ride.

Also around this time, Depot decided that all female recruits MUST have short hair. Woman could no longer pin their hair up. There were a lot of women who had long hair who were very upset about this sudden change in policy, and no explanation was given for this new rule. Some of the women who were set to graduate within a few months considered quitting the RCMP instead of cutting their hair.

In the end, Depot decided to grandfather the women who had started with long hair, but after this group of women, all women would have to cut their hair short. Earlier, a woman in my troop decided to colour her hair from brown to red. It wasn't the bright red you might see today, just a touch of red. As soon as the Drill Instructor noticed her hair, though, she was ordered to dye it back to her natural colour. Women were not allowed to wear makeup and they had to keep their fingernails cut short.

ABOUT half way through training, we had been asked to list which three provinces we would like to be posted to, but were told that we could not be transferred back to our home province. Being from New Brunswick I wanted to get as close to home as possible, so I asked for Nova Scotia, Prince Edward Island or Newfoundland. I was told that Prince Edward Island is considered part of Nova Scotia and that they weren't taking any recruits, so I had to pick another option. I told them I wanted to keep Nova Scotia on the list, in case things changed, and added Quebec to my choices. But I was told I wasn't bilingual enough to go to Quebec, so I picked Ontario, just moving my way across the provinces nearest home. So my final list ended up being Nova Scotia, Ontario and Newfoundland, but there was no guarantee that I would get any of my choices.

I also learned that, aside from personal preferences, another factor involved in posting officers was the policy that, if male and female members were dating or even married, they could NOT be stationed together in the same detachment. No one ever explained the reasons for this.

One of the women that I had become friends with was told before she was hired that she would be posted back to Toronto with her husband. She had it in writing. Instead the RCMP sent her to British Columbia. For over a year and a half she worked in British Columbia and her husband in Toronto. Ultimately though, she was transferred to a detachment in Ontario. I thought this policy was outrageous for her. This was 1987 not 1887!

Another couple I'd met in Depot would also be kept apart by this policy. A woman and a man in two of the other troops were engaged. The man, whose name was Dan, was being posted to New Brunswick, in my hometown of Neguac in fact, and his fiancée was posted three hours away. I was introduced to Dan by a mutual friend and told him a bit about Neguac and the detachment members I knew. I told him it was a very busy detachment, but that he would learn a lot there, and encouraged him to look up my parents when he got there.

After I'd graduated, I went home for two weeks before going to my posting. I met up with Dan and introduced him to my parents. He gradually became a part of our family, being invited over for Christmas dinners, Easter, Thanksgiving. Whenever Dan wanted a coffee, the door was always open. That is what being part of the Mountie family was all about. Many RCMP officers arrived at their postings in provinces where they had no family or friends, and the relationships with other members were all they had for support.

ABOUT a month before graduating, we were told which provinces we'd be posted to. The postings were announced in front of the entire troop and I remember there being more tears than joy. From our troop, four recruits were posted to Newfoundland, two to Quebec, eighteen to Ontario, two to Manitoba and two to British Columbia. Everyone was surprised at how many recruits were going to Ontario.

Then around three weeks before the end of training, we received our detachments. I was going to Niagara. One instructor called me out: "Breau, who do you know to get Niagara?" suggesting I'd had some sort of connection that got me assigned there.

I answered truthfully, "No one Corporal".

When I phoned my parents to tell them my posting, they thought I had said Grand Falls, which was in New Brunswick. I had to keep repeating to them that I was going to Niagara Falls in Ontario. They were also disappointed to learn that recruits could not be posted back to their home provinces.

DURING the week or two before the end of training, our instructors told us about some of the practical jokes and pranks the detachment would play on the new members. They showed us a video of a new member who was told to go to the morgue and take the fingerprints of a deceased person. What the new member didn't know was that it was his trainer lying on the slab. The trainer had placed his hands in ice so that they would feel cold, and as the new member tried to take the fingerprints, the body moved.

The new member jumped back and looked at the coroner with confusion on his face. Then when he bravely tried to take fingerprints from the other hand, the body sat up and came to life. In the video we could see the new recruit scream and run out of the room.

We had been warned. Be on guard when you get to your new detachment!

MY parents flew out to Regina to attend my graduation, which was an emotional day for me. The saddest part was saying goodbye to my troop mates who had been my family for the last six months.

I loved being at Depot. Except for the typing and the tear gas, I'd loved every part of it! It had been the best experience of my life. I loved the structure of it, the learning and the feeling that I was growing into the strong, independent person I dreamed of being. I remember receiving my badge and thinking, *How could I ever give it back?*

After the graduation weekend was over, I packed up what little I had, and we flew home to New Brunswick. I did a lot of reflecting when I was home, knowing I would probably never live in New Brunswick again. In some ways, it was sad having to say goodbye to my family again, but it was exciting too.

After two weeks, I flew to Toronto to start my life as an RCMP officer.

Chapter Nine

❦

WHEN I FOUND OUT I was being posted to Niagara Falls, I received a note from my trainer. He asked if I would be buying a house or renting, and wanted to know when I would be arriving. I told him that I would be flying to Toronto, leaving my car in New Brunswick so that my mom could have it, and would be looking to rent an apartment and purchase a cheap car.

He suggested, "You should rent a car from the airport and take the QEW". "What's the "QEW"?"

"The Queen Elizabeth Way," he explained.

Then when I asked him what the "Queen Elizabeth Way" was, he decided he'd better come and pick me up.

SO on August 3, 1987, I arrived at Toronto Airport.

My trainer picked me up at the airport as promised and drove me to Niagara Detachment. When we arrived, he walked me through the detachment, where I met a lot of people. I also noticed that no one was wearing a uniform. When I asked my trainer about this, he said that officers worked in plain clothes in this detachment. Not sure what that meant, I asked for clarification.

"No one wears a uniform—they wear business clothes and drive unmarked cars."

I asked, "What kind of work do they do?"

"We deal with immigration and smuggling."

We had talked about that in training, but I still wasn't sure what it all meant. Although they'd also taught us about drugs, I was the only recruit in my class who had never seen a marihuana plant. But that was that about to change. I was really confused.

Nothing was what I had expected it would be like, but I was ready and willing to start my new life with my new RCMP family, or so I thought.

We left the detachment with another member, Jim, who was 6'2", about two hundred pounds and had long hair, for a Mountie that is.

We drove to motel called Harvey Ho's, which ended up being a bar. My trainer and the other member sat down and ordered a pitcher of beer and three glasses. Initially, I refused a glass, but both officers insisted that I drink with them.

Was this my prank? Were they testing me?

Not wanting to be caught in a prank, I refused, but they kept insisting.

Eventually, I took a drink and they didn't say anything. Apparently, this was not a prank, and I would not lose my job for taking a drink.

They just continued drinking.

I found out later that the detachment had indeed pulled several pranks on new members. In one instance, they made a new member go out to put up the flag. But it turned out we didn't have control over the flag as we rented the space. Another time, a corporal dressed up as the detachment commander had a secretary sitting on his lap, as he welcomed the new member to the detachment.

The worst prank I'd heard of, though, was when a member had asked permission to marry, and the detachment told him that he must submit a sperm sample before the RCMP would allow it. And he did!

LATER that night, my trainer brought me over to Jim's house and there I met both of their wives. Jim's wife asked me if I played softball, and when I told her that I did, she suggested that I could play ball on her local team the following year. Well that was a year away, but at least I had something to look forward to. Later Jim would tell me" What happens at work stays at work!. Funny enough, Jim's wife said " What happens at the ball diamond stays at the ball diamond!" In other words, keep your mouth shut! Turned out to be great advice.

MY first problem at Niagara Detachment was, of course, that all of the clothes I owned were my uniforms. I didn't have a lot of business clothes and had no idea that Ontario didn't have the uniform policing I was familiar with in New Brunswick.

The RCMP does what they call "Contract Policing" in every province and territory except for Ontario and Quebec, which means the federal government signs a "contract" with the provinces and territories to have the RCMP as the Police in that area. But in Ontario and Quebec, the RCMP do what is called "Federal Policing" since both provinces have their own provincial police and municipal police, and the RCMP work on Federal offences such as Organized Crime, Frauds, Custom and Excise (smuggling), Immigration, Federal Enforcement Section (all other federal statues) and Drug investigations. In Federal Policing, members wear business attire also known as plain clothes sections. In the Drug Section, business attire is required when attending court, but the clothing is much more casual due to the type of work being conducted. Plain clothes does not necessarily mean Undercover officers. An Undercover officer works undercover to purchased drugs, where a plain clothes officer may provide the undercover officer protection, conduct surveillance and other duties. At first, I didn't know the difference, but I would soon learn.

In Depot, the lecture on Federal Policing had been just a few hours long, as almost all recruits would be stationed in a Contract (Uniform) Policing position. So this situation I found myself in was unexpectedly different and quite intimidating. During my recruit field training, I would working for a short time in each of these sections, in order to get familiarized with what each section did. It was going to be a long learning curve.

ON my second day, I was shown around the detachment. I noticed that my mailbox already had two files in it. My heart began racing. They already had work for me to do! It turned out the files were subpoenas that I had to serve, something I had never done before. It seemed really daunting at the time, but they proved to be one of the easiest things to do.

IT soon became apparent that I was the only female member at this detachment. In the beginning, I thought I might be the first female member ever to be posted in Niagara, but later found out that I was the second.

I was introduced to the first female member stationed at Niagara, a few months after arriving. She worked at a local clothing store. She revealed to me that she left the force after enduring months of harassment from the male members. This was a very disturbing thing for me to hear.

WITHIN a day or two, I was taken out for a drive in one of our unmarked cars it was like a Dodge K-Car—no lights, no sirens, no air conditioning, roll-down windows and propane powered. Just an extremely plain car.

The only cool thing about it was when the member showed me the police radio. It looked like any other car radio, but when he pulled the radio cover down, there hiding behind it was a police radio.

Wow! It was just like on TV!

There was, however, no regular radio in the car. Meaning, no music.

AFTER the first couple of days of getting myself settled at the detachment, I was left on my own. My trainer's wife was pregnant and due soon, and within a couple of weeks, he was busy dealing with his newborn son. So I would arrive at the detachment every morning, read policy all day, then go home to my hotel. Any social activity consisted of going with the male officers to a bar to drink beer and watch baseball on the television.

Drinking seemed to be their main form of entertainment.

ON one occasion, I was assigned to work a Red Serge duty. That means that the RCMP had received a request to have a member attend a public event wearing the famous Red Serge. A male member was dressed up in his Red Serge and I was in mine. At the event, a woman asked to have her picture taken with the Mountie. The member stood beside her and I stood on the other side of her.

Then she said, "No not you, I don't want my picture taken with the Salvation Army, just the Mountie".

I was humiliated that the female version of the uniform was not even recognized as belonging to a Mountie. It wouldn't be until 1990 that I would receive the same uniform as the male members.

MEANWHILE, I kept my head down, read policy, and began to set up my life in my new city. Within a couple of days, I'd purchased a used Dodge K-Car. It had a red interior and no air conditioning, but at least now I could drive myself to and from work. Although my trainer had made some attempts to locate an apartment for me, there were no apartments available, so I was forced to live in a hotel for a month.

I eventually did find an apartment available on September 1, so I bought a bed and a couch with a pull-out bed and had the delivery date for the same date. I also bought a used rocking chair and a stool, and one of the secretaries let me borrow a card table and two chairs so I could have somewhere to sit and eat.

So come the first of September, there I was sitting on my rocking chair in the middle of a nearly empty apartment, ready to take on the world.

Chapter Ten

🍁

SOON AFTER ARRIVING AT NIAGARA Detachment, a member invited me to lunch, and I was glad that someone had asked me to join them. During the whole lunch hour, he told me that females should not be allowed to join the RCMP as Regular Members. He told me that he'd gone through Depot during the same time as the first female troop and said those females had "slept" their way through Depot. I sat there, shocked and speechless, for an hour and listened to him berate female members. He stated the RCMP could even pay us more as long as females were not Regular Members.

I nervously told him that I was not part of that first female troop and suggested that he give me a chance to prove myself.

This would not be the last time I would have to prove myself worthy of being an RCMP officer. I was always introduced as a "female" member, never as a member. The distinction was not uncommon. Even female officers with the Niagara Regional Police Service were referred to as "PWs", Police Women. It would take years before we became known as "members".

Some members initially referred to me as "PC", Police Chick. It also wasn't uncommon for other visible members to be referred to as a "Black Member", or a "Native Member". All I had ever wanted was to simply be a member, but it turned out there was going to be nothing simple about it.

ANOTHER recruit, who had arrived at Niagara about three months before I did, took me out to show me around. Once again, I was just thrilled to be out of the office. This member drove me around Niagara Falls, the whole time pointing out restaurants, bars and stores that would give police discounts. *Really? Where did he learn this?* How to use your badge to gain favour, put your business card in your windshield so you don't get a ticket. *Where did they hire this member?*

Within a few months of that tour of the town, a local magazine interviewed that same new recruit. In the article, he stated that members who worked in Contract Policing had better chances of meeting girls. He joked that it was much harder here because he worked undercover.

I was so upset that I photocopied the article and put it in each employee's mail slot. After that, every time I walked past his desk, he would lower his head so that he didn't have to talk or look at me. I called him the Ostrich!

A few months later, when I worked at the G7 Summit, I worked with his brother who wasn't much different than he was. It was a type of officer that I would encounter rather often.

THE one member who seemed to be paying attention to me, ended up offering the wrong kind of attention. He would look at my breasts when speaking to me and, as I walked away, he would look at my backside.

During my third or fourth week at this detachment, he asked me to come into his office. As I entered, he was closing the door behind me. Then he grabbed me and kissed me on the lips. I broke away from his grip and stuck my foot in the door, preventing it from closing. I told him if he ever touched me again, I would defend myself and that I would tell his wife.

At first, I was shocked, then I was angry. How dare he do that to me!

I couldn't believe that a fellow officer had attacked me and that he did so in the detachment! If he was willing to attack me at the office, what if he were to follow me home, I wondered.

I reported the incident, but nothing was done about it. I was merely told to stay away from him. Since we worked in the same small office, that was not a solution, but it was the only one offered to me. After that, I no longer felt safe around him at work, and I felt like I was on my own in dealing with it. I had to constantly watch where I went and make sure to never be caught alone with him or anyone else.

This pattern of behaviour continued unchecked. He continued to stare at my breasts and backside, and I did everything I could not to be left alone with him. I stayed away from his office area for fear that he would attack me again.

At detachment functions where alcohol was consumed, he would become very aggressive and make passes at me. But he became smarter about it. He would rub up against me, look over my shoulder and make comments that only I could hear.

He would also do the same thing when I was in the office. We had one computer in the bullpen area, and when I was running a CPIC check, he would stand behind me and reach over my shoulder to point at something on the screen and rub my shoulder then rub my breast with his forearm. I felt helpless to control the situation and he continued these advances for years to come.

AFTER a month or so, a second female member was stationed at Niagara. She approached me and told me she was very uncomfortable around the same member as he was staring at her breasts and treating her the same way he was treating me. I felt it was my duty to try to protect her and tried to make sure she was never alone with him.

Many years later, after he'd separated from his wife, he approached me and told me that he was now available. In all that time, he had not learned a thing!

*

WHEN I did my rotation in the Fraud Section, I felt as if I were treated like a secretary. They gave me cassette tapes, which contained interviews, and asked me to transcribe them.

In their minds, this was a job that was beneath a male officer and could only be done by a woman. I wondered, who had done it in the days before female recruits were hired, but I kept my mouth shut and my head down.

IN 1987, the only computers in the detachment were assigned to the secretaries. I think there were only four computers in the detachment at that time. I didn't even know how to turn one on, since all our typing was done on a typewriter. When I had to type a search warrant, I would put carbon paper between two forms (so that we could have a copy of the warrant) and type the warrant out. I used a lot of White-Out as I made lots of mistakes! Did I mention I couldn't type?

OF the more than forty members and employees in the detachment, only one member and one secretary ever invited me to their homes. No one else bothered to go out of their way to make me feel like a member at all.

One secretary did do the most to make me feel welcomed. She would invite to her home on weekends for dinner and to watch football with her family, and would come to treat me like family. This was very different from my treatment by the detachment in New Brunswick where I'd been treated like family even before I became a member.

DISCRIMINATION against female members was not limited to inside the detachment itself. Some members felt they should not tell their wives that a female was now working at the office. This became an issue when I was asked to bring a member's paycheque to his house while he was away on a training course. It happened to be that same member who'd taken me for lunch so he could tell me why I shouldn't be a Regular Member of the RCMP.

I called his house and advised his wife that I would be stopping by to drop off her husband's cheque. She asked who I was, and I told her, adding that I would be at her house in about twenty minutes. When I arrived, there were four ladies sitting in the living room. I was invited in, and that's when the questions started. The wives had no idea that I was a member and working with their husbands, and they didn't appear to be happy about it either.

It was a very uncomfortable situation.

ONE member let me know that he'd told his wife about me and wanted to invite me over, but at the time his wife did not want anything to do with me. Another member that I worked with had bought his wife some perfume for Christmas. He had sprayed it on his arm so that he could smell it. When she smelled the perfume on him, she accused him of cheating on her. She blamed me. She thought I was just there to get a husband.

That night, he made his wife open her Christmas present. A bottle of perfume. I never wore perfume. In the end, she would apologize to me.

Chapter Eleven

🍁

WHEN MY ROTATION TOOK ME to the Drug Section, the sergeant in charge of the section called me into his office, closed the door and told me that females should be bare foot and pregnant in the kitchen but not in the RCMP and certainly not in his Drug Section. I would only be in the Drug Section for six weeks as part of my rotation. I could make it six weeks.

The best part about working in the Drug Section, though, was that I could wear regular clothes. No more dressing up! Jeans and sneakers were much more comfortable then business attire and high heel shoes.

I was asked to try to buy some drugs. I was chosen because there were so few female officers that no one would suspect I was a cop. Although I had no experience in this area and had never been trained for this type of work, I wanted to fit in, so I agreed to try it.

I remember very clearly the first time I tried to buy drugs.

It was dark out. The house I approached was an A-frame and I remember looking up and seeing the cobwebs over the front door. My body was shaking, I was so nervous, and I'm sure my voice was shaking too. My heart was pounding fast and hard.

I knocked on the door and a woman answered. I asked to buy drugs. And then she slammed the door in my face!

After several attempts, over a period of time, I made my first purchase of marihuana. I had been given $100 and told to buy an ounce of mari-huana, so I drove the car to the address I was given, got out of the car and walked up to the front door. I was given his first name and told to say that a cab driver had told me I could buy some weed from him.

I knocked on the front door and this time a male answered. When I told him a cab driver sent me to him for weed, he asked me how much I wanted. I asked for an ounce. He told me to wait there and went to get the drugs.

He came back with a clear plastic bag with some greenish plant-like material in it and said it'd be $300. I said, "I only wanted an ounce."

"That's what you got, an ounce".

Embarrassed, I asked how much I could get for $100.

"That would buy a quarter of an ounce," he said and proceeded to separate the drugs and weigh it in front of me.

Then I returned to the detachment and handed over the drugs, letting them know that an ounce was $300. It was obvious that the Section was out of touch with the street prices.

I must admit, I felt like I had just won the lottery. I was so excited that I'd managed to buy some drugs as an undercover officer! Me!

The Drug Section was pleased, After I was rotated to another section,they continued to ask me to come out to purchase drugs, which I agreed to do on my own time since this helped to pass the time as I had no friends and didn't know anyone in the community. I also wanted very badly to be a part of the RCMP family and would do whatever it took to be accepted.

THE more drug purchases I made, the more I felt that the members were accepting me, and possibly even respecting me. I didn't even question the fact that I was being asked to do this on my own time. I was so proud to become a Mountie, but now I couldn't tell anyone that I was because it could compromise my security as an undercover officer. I understood why but felt disappointed just the same.

Besides being a female officer, another amazing tool was the belief among drug dealers that, if they asked you if you were a police officer, you'd have to tell the truth and say YES. Evidently, that was the case in the United States. Somehow the word spread and it was widely believed. In fact, I was asked that question almost every single time I purchased drugs, but of course, in Canada, that's not the law, and so I would lie and say that I wasn't a cop and people sold me drugs.

The first thing I usually heard after they were arrested was, "I asked you if you were a cop and you said NO!" Boy were they pissed off! Happily, that urban legend worked in my favour for almost a year.

THAT first year, I went to the Detachment's Christmas party, which was the time I would first meet most of the members' wives. At one point, I was in a washroom stall when a couple of the members' wives came in, not knowing I was in there and, for no good reason, were talking about me. What they said was not nice.

I walked out of the stall, calmly washed my hands and walked out of the washroom without saying a word. One of the wives was the one whose husband's pay cheque I had delivered to her home. Instead of being welcomed into the "family", I was beginning to feel clearly unwelcome.

Soon after that, the Drug Section was preparing to execute a search warrant on a possible drug dealer, and I was told to get my gun and come along. I also grabbed my bulletproof vest. Once in the car, the other officer pointed and said, "You're not going to wear that!" referring to my vest, and asked if I was afraid. Feeling too intimidated to protest, I left the vest in the back seat of the car. I didn't want them to think I was afraid.

When we arrived at the residence, I was told to stay in the car. When I said that I wanted to participate in the raid, he told me again to stand by the car. I had to stand there and watch the big brave men of the Drug Section approach the residence while I was not allowed to participate.

A few seconds after they entered the front door, a man came running from the back of the house. It was the suspect whose picture I'd been shown during the briefing and he was running straight toward me. As I had been trained to do, I pulled out my gun, pointed it at him and hollered very loudly, "Get down or I'll shoot!"

Luckily, he stopped and the brave members of Drug Section came running out. It was like an episode of Keystone Cops—the tiny little inexperienced girl stopped the big bad drug dealer all by herself.

After that, I was never told to stay in the car again.

ON January 15, 1988, I completed my six months recruit Field Training. My training was officially over. I'd obtained an A on my final exam and was given an A+ for my great attitude. Along with the end of training came my very first pay raise. Then on February 29, I was permanently transferred to the Drug Section. I was sitting across from a French member, so I asked him if he was upset with having a female member in the Section.

The words he said next helped me to understand how to make it in the Drug Section. He said, "I don't care if you're a female or not, as long as you do your fair share of the work." That would be easy I thought. It wasn't.

WITHIN a short period of time, I began to observe activities committed by the Drug Section members that were very embarrassing and degrading to women in general and especially to me. During search warrants, the members of the Section would search for drugs, but if they came across stuff like porn or sex toys, they would leave them out on display in the room where they were found. Usually the items such as vibrators, underwear, or pictures were set out on top of the suspect's bed just to embarrass me. Some of the members even took these items back to the detachment.

At Christmas, the Drug Section set up a small Christmas tree that they would decorate with the items and pictures they'd taken. On one occasion, another Section received a call from the border that customs had seized pornographic videos. They were illegal to import into Canada, but the members took turns copying the videos for their own use.

AROUND this time, I also became aware of the "suspect book". This was a photo album filled with nude pictures of drug suspects. These pictures had been taken from the houses of individuals and put into a photo album that was kept in the corporal's office. When a visiting member attended the detachment, the corporal would make a big show of having them come in to look at the suspect book.

I found this extremely unprofessional and a violation of the suspects' rights. I was so embarrassed when I saw this happening on more than one occasion that I told them they shouldn't do that. They just laughed at me and continued on with this inappropriate behaviour.

At one point, I was so upset over the way the members were bragging about the suspect book that I hid it in an empty exhibit locker. I was so tired of watching the members laugh and joke about the photos that I couldn't take it anymore. It was degrading to the victims and I found it very degrading to me as a female to have to put up with this type of unprofessional activity.

The members noticed right away that the book had gone missing, searching the office looking for it. I overheard them saying, "What if someone sent it to CROPS[6].

---

6   CROPS Criminal Operations. CROPS is where Senior management is located and they would investigate any complaints of wrong doing

They believed another female member of the Drug Section had taken the book and made a complaint against them, and they were worried about being investigated.

Later that night, a male member arrived at my personal residence to ask if I knew where the book was. He said he'd overheard me saying one day I would get rid of that book, and told me that the Drug Section members had called him in and questioned him.

Evidently, they'd been searching the office and found some of the pictures from the suspect book in his desk. While he admitted that he had taken some of the pictures from the book for his own use, he hadn't taken the book itself and didn't know where it was. They didn't believe him and told him if he didn't have the book back in the office by Monday morning, they would have him fired.

Although I felt awful about what he was going through, I denied knowing where the book was. I didn't trust him well enough to tell him the truth. I decided that I had better put the photo album back as I hadn't meant for this situation to get this far out of hand. I had just wanted the members to stop what they were doing.

That same night, around 1:00 am, I went to the detachment, as I knew the office would be empty, and this was before cameras were installed in detachments. I wore a set of gloves as I didn't want to leave fingerprints and get caught returning the book. Unlocking the door of the detachment, I walked in the dark to the exhibit room. I opened the exhibit locker where I had hidden the photo album and—

It was gone! Damn! Now what?

I was scared. I didn't know what to do. So, I left the detachment, locked it up and went home.

I didn't sleep that night because I was too worried about where the book

51

had gone and who might have taken it. I'd put a member in a difficult position and now I didn't know what to do to help him out of the mess I had put him in.

The next day, I went to see my best friend, told her what I'd done and how I only wanted the members to stop what they were doing and how they had threatened a male member. After much thought and discussion, I decided to admit to taking the book to save the member from the harassment he had been going through. I would have to take my chances that I might get transferred out of the detachment or even worse, fired.

On Monday, I told the sergeant that I'd hidden the album. Unexpectedly, he told me that someone else had also admitted to hiding the album, that the book had been located and it would be kept in a more discreet location.

I was terrified that the Drug Section members would turn against me, and that I'd be forced out of the Section. To this day, though, I believe the sergeant didn't tell the Section members that it was me who'd hidden the book since there was never any retaliation against me for it.

Nonetheless, I felt very badly that my actions had caused so much stress and worry for that member who'd been accused of taking the book. He had a wife and two young kids to support.

Shortly after that incident, he'd asked for a transfer to BC and was soon gone. Recalling this, I still feel badly for him, but I realize that, at that time, this was taken as acceptable behaviour in our Drug Section and no one was willing to put a stop to it. It wouldn't be the last time that I'd witness this sort of behaviour going unchecked.

IN these early days, it wasn't unusual for posters showing bikini-clad women, known as "Sunshine Girls", to be displayed in the drug squad area of the office. This created a definite male atmosphere that often led me to wonder what I'd gotten myself into by joining the RCMP. The Mounties in my hometown had been so nice and had done a lot to help me join their ranks, yet the Mounties at this detachment seemed so distant. It was an old boys club here and they made it clear that women were not invited.

Chapter Twelve

🍁

THE DRUG SECTION WORKED SHIFTS, one week of days followed by one week of nights. During the night shifts that started at 4:00 pm, I would eat my supper in a restaurant or fast food place, as no time was allotted to go back home or back to the detachment to eat. We did a lot of surveillance and were constantly sitting in cars, often eating our meals in our cars too.

It was a constant challenge for me to find a washroom. The guys could use the outdoors, but I couldn't do that, even though they told me to. Many times, I would have to hold my bladder until the surveillance was over or they could break me free to go to a washroom. Ultimately, I'd avoid drinking fluids just so that I didn't have to go to the washroom during my shifts. Sadly, that turned out to be the same for most of my career.

AT this time in my early career, it frequently seemed that I was left completely on my own without any guidance. One time, I was made the Exhibit Officer on a small marihuana plant seizure. I seized the drugs and sealed them in an exhibit bag, then placed it in a temporary exhibit locker. A few days later, I needed to send a sample to the drug lab for testing, but when the sergeant removed the exhibit bag, all that was left was a soupy substance. I had no idea that the plants would rot in the plastic bag. Lesson learned. This was well-known by the other members, but an example of the kind of thing nobody would make the effort to explain to me beforehand.

SHORTLY after I was stationed in the Drug Section, we started a Joint Forces Drug Team, which included officers from the Niagara Regional Police Service. Four Niagara officers started working out of the RCMP detachment and fortunately one of these officers was a female. I was paired up with her and we would go around making drug purchases. It was a relief having another woman to work with. She had done some previous undercover work and we were paired up so she could teach me how to get better at it. Together we bought a lot of drugs.

Watching her in action, how cool she was and her "gift of the gab" gave me insights into how to "handle" the men in the Section. The Niagara guys treated her with respect, and she didn't take any shit from anyone. I wanted to be more like her in that way, but acting like that made her appear to be "rough around the edges". I often worried that I might turn out the way too if I were to adopt her methods for commanding respect from my fellow officers.

DURING this period of time it seemed as though every person we ever bought drugs from was killed. One fellow was killed weeks after he'd been arrested for selling us drugs when someone stabbed him repeatedly with two swords. I remember seeing his photos and feeling bad for him. The members, though, jokingly called him Shish Kabob—police have a strange sense of humour. It was an awful way to die.

Another man was shot to death in a strip club, shot in both knees then twice in the chest. It was clear that the violence in the drug trade was escalating, but thankfully for us, they were killing each other and not the police.

I started working a three month undercover job in St. Catharines in January 1988. By this point, I had only one year of service, which included my time at Depot and six months of training at the detachment, and although I wasn't a trained UCO,[7] I was allowed to perform some of their duties. Before starting, the supervisor in charge of the team asked me if I had any street clothes. Not knowing how exactly I should dress, he mentioned his son had a black leather jacket that might fit me and make me look a little tougher. He brought it into work and I wore that jacket for the next two to three years.

But it was apparent to everyone at the time that I didn't look like a street person. I appeared too clean, I had good teeth and didn't have dark circles under my eyes, even though I would get cigarette ashes and rub some under my eyes and on my teeth. I also didn't comb my hair, trying to make it look unkempt so I could look the part.

In addition to changing my appearance, I had to learn to swear and talk like the people I met, learn the street terms for drugs and try not to walk or talk like a cop. The hardest part was over-thinking it. In my mind I knew I was a cop and often worried that the suspects would know or find out that I was.

When I went into a bar, I would order a rum and coke as a drink. Because I was nervous, I drank it way too quickly and thought to myself, *I can't keep drinking these.*

I switched to beer. A bottle of beer took longer to drink and I didn't like the taste of it as much. Another great part about beer was that I could pour the beer down the sink in the bathroom if no one was there, then fill the bottle with water. No one could tell I was drinking water and I could always refill it again so that it always looked like I had something to drink.

One of the difficult parts of being by yourself in a bar is that guys hit

---

7   Undercover operator

on you. They want to buy you drinks and put their hands on you. There were even a few nights I had to hold someone away from me as he tried to plant a kiss on my mouth. This was something the male members never had to deal with.

Another problem was that we targeted an area that was well known for drug activity, and one of the bars was a local strip club. It was always uncomfortable for me to enter these premises because it didn't seem normal for a girl to go into a strip club by herself. I was the only one who questioned this or seemed to care, but in my mind, I didn't think that made any sense. At least there was a member of my team who would also enter the bar so that I had some kind of backup in case anything went wrong.

I usually hung around the pool tables that had the best lighting in the bar. I'd play pool and meet people and eventually ask them where I could buy drugs. It seemed the pool tables were the place to be.

ONCE I'd made a buy at one bar, I'd walk down the block to another bar and attempt to make another buy. I had a system. The first drug purchase would go in my left front pants pocket, the second in my right pants pocket. One night, I had to put the drugs into my jacket pockets too as I'd made more than two purchases. And so, it went, night after night, entering bars and buying drugs.

I learned something new every time—when I made my first buy, I'd tried to hand the dealer my money over the top of the table. He hissed, "No! Under the table! You don't want anyone to see!" He was teaching me how to play it cool. Little did he know I was the cop.

I'd wanted to hand the money over the top of the table so that my cover team could see I was making a deal. Instead I had to remember to behave like a criminal and not a cop. I started to act as if I was looking around too to make sure nobody saw us doing a drug deal. I was learning as I went along.

*

ANOTHER night as we entered the strip bar, my cover man went in first and a few minutes later I followed. The place was packed with women! That night the male Chippendales were dancing. Male strippers!

I laughed inwardly, thinking that finally he got to feel the way I did, outnumbered by the opposite sex. There he was sitting all by himself in the back of the bars, the only man in a room full of women. Karma! I laughed about that one for a long time.

ON another night, I entered the bar down the street and went to the room of a guy I was buying drugs from. As we were getting ready to make the deal, two men entered the room. They said they had just committed a break and enter of a patron who'd happened to be drinking downstairs in the bar. They said they had two rifles they wanted to sell and if they couldn't sell the guns, they were going to rob the Subway store down the street to get money for drugs.

My heart was pounding. Thinking quickly, I said my boyfriend liked guns and that he might buy them. I asked how much they wanted for the guns and they said $150. I told them to wait there and I would go get my boyfriend.

I left the bar and ran as fast as I could to where my cover team was located. My heart still racing, I told them about the guns. They agreed we couldn't leave the guns in their hands and needed to prevent the armed robbery.

With one of the guys acting as my boyfriend, we got the money and returned to the room. We purchased the guns and then returned to the Niagara police station to hand them over to the Break & Entry Section. We'd solved a break and entry before it had even been reported and prevented the risk of injury or death that night. What an amazing feeling!

*

I'D purchased drugs from individuals at the bar, but also from a couple that hung out at the bar. At first, the man was hesitant to sell to me since he didn't know who I was. His girlfriend vouched for me, though, stating I was cool and that she'd seen me several times in the bar so at last he sold me cocaine.

On a later date, he told me he could spot a cop a mile away. The whole time I was thinking, *Well then, thank God I'm right next to him and not a mile away.* He tested me on several occasions always asking me to do drugs in front of him. Of course, I always had a reason why I couldn't. I was going to see my boyfriend and I didn't want his parents to see me high. Snorting cocaine would make me throw up. Cocaine gave me nosebleeds. I used needles and injected cocaine.

I used whatever excuses I could come up with, knowing that using cocaine even once, a person could possibility overdose and die. Unless he held a gun to my head, I would NEVER use drugs, but he kept testing me.

Luckily, his girlfriend always supported me. When the undercover operation was completed and it was time to do the takedowns, he was furious with her as they both were arrested and transported to jail.

In all, over the course of three months, I'd purchased drugs from eleven drug traffickers, and a total of twenty-two charges were laid.

Chapter Thirteen

🍁

THE LONGER I WORKED IN this section, the more I learned about the various drugs, how to use them, and some of their effects. As I continued to work undercover, this would help me to improve my knowledge and ability to learn what excuses to use and how to sound like a drug user.

When they arrested the guy I'd been buying cocaine from, and where I had purchased the guns, his arms were full of needle marks where he'd injected the cocaine. Months later during his trial, he marched right up to me at court. I thought he was going to try to start a fight with me. Instead he stopped, rolled up his sleeves and said, "Look—no track marks.[8] You saved my life when you arrested me. I have been clean for four months."

That was an amazing moment for me. I'd never looked at it that way before—that I was actually saving a drug addict's life by putting him in prison.

AFTER the takedown, word had gotten out that I was a cop in that part of St. Catharines, and as I would soon learn, I had to keep moving around. So we moved toward Niagara Falls, targeting another area where drugs were commonly being sold. Some of these bars where I purchased drugs were very dirty and run down. I also purchased some drugs from a few

---

8   Injection marks

prostitutes on the street.

One night, we received a tip that one of the local girls was in possession of cocaine. The tipster was her boyfriend. He told us that she'd hidden the drugs in her vagina. When we located her and I made a purchase of a gram of coke, the guys grabbed and arrested her. Then we took her to the cells and I conducted a strip search.

It was my job to tell the suspect to bend over and spread her legs. The smell was awful. I could see a piece of plastic hanging in her vaginal area, though, so I asked her to pull it out. She refused.

I placed her back into her cell and told her the water was turned off and she was on video surveillance in her cell. Then I met with the team and told them I could see the plastic bag, but there was no way I was going to put my hands in there to pull it out even with gloves on! So we agreed to take her to the hospital and have a doctor take it out.

Once at the hospital, the suspect refused to let the doctor touch her, even though we told her she could overdose if she didn't take the drugs out. But the doctor told us that once a patient refused treatment there was nothing he could do. Out of alternative options, we took her back to the cells.

I called my boss to advise him of the issue and he said, "Well she has to pee sometime."

I didn't think he'd heard me so I repeated the fact that the drugs were in her vagina.

"I heard you the first time," he said and repeated that I was to shut off the water and just wait. When I hung up the phone, I just shook my head. Evidently, he didn't understand female anatomy.

At this point, I thought my best chance was to bluff her, so I told her we were preparing a search warrant to conduct a body cavity search, which would give the doctor permission to remove the drugs. Thankfully, she believed me and when I took her to a private room she removed the drugs. What a relief for me!

*

DURING one search warrant, we did a high-risk entry. Unfortunately, the door did not open after we hit it with the battering ram, and when we finally entered the house, the suspect kept yelling at his girlfriend to flush the drugs.

Upon hearing the toilet flush, we ran into the bathroom and there on top of the water, twirling around was a plastic bag full of air and cocaine. There was so much air in the bag that it wouldn't go down the drain! Score one for the good guys.

ONE guy I was buying drugs from was a young offender. The RCMP did not normally allow us to target young offenders, but this was an exception since this guy was a dealer and was selling to school kids. Luckily, at this point in my career, I looked young enough that I was able to convince him to sell me drugs.

One time I showed up to buy some marihuana from him and he had a black eye and looked like he'd been in a fight. I asked him what had happened and he told me that he'd been beaten up because he had run out of dope and needed to pay his supplier, so he had taken some dried dog droppings, froze it, cut it up into small pieces, wrapped it up and sold it as hashish.

Apparently one of his customers had tried to smoke it, realized of course that it was fake and beat him up. Must have been some really bad shit! I would use that story a lot when I was lecturing kids about drugs. Some stories you just can't make up.

ONE of the prostitutes that I had dealings with, I called "The Kid". She'd been at some of the houses where we had conducted raids. During one of those raids, she approached me to tell me where the drugs were in exchange for getting the kids out of the house and calling Children's Services. She wanted the kids to be taken away from their mother.

In the living room was a family portrait of the mother and the three kids. When I asked the suspect who the woman in the picture was, she answered "Me".

She had aged about thirty years in appearance after just one year of being addicted to methenamine. She'd lost a lot of weight, her skin was a greyish colour, her face was covered with open sores, her teeth were rotten and she had several track marks on her arm. It was her own children she wanted removed from their mother.

One of the children even begged me to take them away from her. I did call Children's Services, but they refused to attend. I was devastated, and nobody in her family was happy about it either. As I was leaving, she said she wanted to take her kids to McDonald's so I gave her twenty dollars to buy them food. I have a soft spot for kids.

IT was hard to leave them in this situation. When I had called Children's Services that day and requested that they attend the residence, I'd informed them that there were no beds or food in the house. A few days later, they reported back that the kids were fine and happy to stay. But when I asked specifically about the lack of beds, they didn't answer.

Had they actually gone into the house, I asked, and they admitted they hadn't. That made me feel frustrated and naïve, as I'd presumed that Children's Services would be there to back me up, and that we were all there to do what was in the best interests of those kids.

*

I stayed in touch with The Kid and she ended up becoming an informant. She would give me information on drug dealers which enabled me to obtain search warrants, seize drugs and lay charges. The Kid wanted to get clean of drugs and went to rehab on several occasions, but failed to stay clean.

I received a call from The Kid one night around 2:00 am. She'd just taken a hit of heroin and thought she was overdosing. I told her to give me her location and I would call an ambulance. She didn't want me to do that because she still had heroin and didn't want to get arrested.

Somehow, she survived that episode and continued to work the streets as a prostitute, even joked about charging ten dollars more for a blowjob if she took her teeth out.

SOON, it seemed as though there was an epidemic of dead bodies in the Niagara region. People were overdosing on heroin. I believe more than twelve people died in the region in a very short period of time.

I always worried about The Kid during this time since heroin was her drug of choice, and while she took the death of her friends very hard, it wasn't hard enough for her to quit using. As it turned out, though, the last drug dealer she turned in before going away to rehab was her supplier. It was the biggest seizure of heroin we had ever made at the time.

EVENTUALLY, I am proud to say, The Kid successfully made it through rehab and has been clean and sober for over twenty years. What surprised me the most, though, is when she confessed what had been the hardest drug to quit, and she would know because she'd done them all. For her, it was cigarettes. You could have knocked me over with a feather.

Ultimately, she was able to get a job, but learning to live a normal life remained difficult. She wasn't accustomed to buying groceries, cooking, renting an apartment and paying her bills. To make matters worse, The Kid was diagnosed with cancer, and treatments were especially difficult because her veins had collapsed from years of injecting drugs. As a credit to her strength, she'd won her war with drugs and went on to win her battle with cancer.

We're still in touch with each other to this day.

Chapter Fourteen

🍁

MY MAIN DUTIES IN THE Drug Section were to work in an undercover capacity buying drugs, then assist in preparing search warrants and make the arrests of the people from whom the drugs were purchased. Our team was so successful that other Drug Sections within Ontario would send their members down to Niagara so that they could see what we were doing and take those skills back to their detachments.

This meant that I would take these members out with me and try to buy drugs, giving them the opportunity to learn what I was doing and get experience buying drugs, taking notes, writing warrants and testifying in court. Officers were being told to learn from me because this was something I excelled at. The team was happy and I felt like a superstar.

One day my commander even approached me and said, "Paulette, why can't all the female members be like you?" I knew I had won him over.

I had arrived! I was one of the boys. It was the happiest time of my career. Sadly I would be short lived.

THERE were a few French-speaking members in Niagara, but we were told not to speak French in the detachment. So we would get together at the detachment on weekends to play ball and do other activities so that we could talk to each other in French. Some of these French-speaking members had their own issues as they had little experience speaking English. Sometimes it made for funny situations.

For instance, one member was in court with his trainer, who had told the member to sit and watch as he gave evidence. At one point, the judge asked the observers in the courtroom if any of them knew the officer giving testimony. The member, who was there only to watch, raised his hand. The judge asked him how he knew the officer, and the member stated that he was his trainer. What the member didn't realize was that the observers were potential jury members and he had just compromised the case.

ANOTHER time, a different French-speaking member was called to testify. After giving his evidence, the judge asked the member to back up his testimony. Not completely understanding the judge's request, the member replied, "But Your Honour, if I back up any further, I will fall out of the witness box!"

One night, that same member was doing surveillance with us. Since the target wasn't moving, we were taking turns going and getting a bite to eat. When it was his turn, he left, but a couple of minutes later we heard him over the police radio, "I'll have a Big Mac, a large fry and a Diet Coke."

I called over the radio, "You're on the wrong microphone!"

Next thing we heard was him repeating his order. I don't remember if he actually got any food that night, but we laughed about that for many years.

ANOTHER night, an undercover officer was going into a strip bar to make a purchase of four ounces of cocaine. After the deal was completed, a search warrant would be executed at the bar, and we would enter the bar, close it and search the building for the drugs. Prior to the search warrant being executed we were advised that the four ounces of cocaine were hidden somewhere in the bar.

As the only female, I was tasked with arresting and searching a woman known only as Miss Nude North America.

I arrested Miss Nude, who was wearing a bikini, and took her to the bathroom to conduct a search. After the search, I told her that we knew there were drugs hidden inside the bar and I asked her if she had anything to confess. She said that she did.

She told me she'd crossed the border and had forgotten to declare something upon entering Canada. I thought she was about to tell me that she had smuggled the drugs across the border, so I asked her to go ahead and tell me what it was.

"I don't want to get in trouble," she said.

"That will depend on what you smuggled across the border."

Miss Nude then grabbed her breasts and said, "These!"

I asked her to clarify what she was saying, and she explained that she'd gotten a "boob job" in the United States and hadn't declared it when she crossed the border.

REALLY!

Miss Nude was an extremely pretty young French Canadian from Quebec, and all the other officers wanted to know how it felt to search Miss Nude North America. When I told them she'd made a confession, they stopped and waited to hear where the drugs were. I told them she confessed to getting breast implants. The drugs were found hidden in the ceiling.

DURING another investigation, I was tasked with obtaining $265,000 in cash to be used as a "flash roll", which is money used to show the drug dealer that we "have" the money, but the money will never leave our hands. Once the suspect is shown the money, it is expected that he will show us the drugs. Once we see the drugs, we conduct a takedown and arrest the suspect.

Getting the money was really cool. Carrying a duffle bag to transport it in, we entered a bank and were escorted to a glassed-in booth. Once there, we signed in and showed our police identification. We were given a pass to wear and then escorted down three floors under the bank where we arrived at another glassed-in booth. We were told to hold our badges up to the camera. Then the door buzzed and we entered.

Once inside I couldn't believe what I was seeing—an actual room full of money! Money was stacked right up to the ceiling. I'd never seen anything like that in my life.

I jokingly asked if I could go into the room and throw the money up into the air but was told I couldn't. Finally, we got down to business.

I presented them with a cheque for the $265,000, and then they took me into a room and asked me what denominations I wanted the cash in. I'd been given no instructions about this, but had been told that I would have to photocopy the money in case of getting robbed, so in order to simplify that part of the job, I said, "How about 265 one-thousand dollar bills?"

The employee left and returned with a big stack of thousand-dollar bills. Using a money-counting machine, she counted out 265 of them. I signed a whole bunch of papers, stuck the money in my pants pockets and headed out of the bank with the empty duffel bag.

When I called my boss to tell him I had the money, he asked me what denominations I'd gotten. Feeling proud of myself, I told him about the thousand dollars bills.

"What!" he said. "Nobody deals in thousand-dollar bills! Go back and get twenties, fifties and hundreds!"

Embarrassed, I returned and obtained the flash roll in the smaller bills as instructed. By the time I left the second time, I had a duffle bag full of money. It took me hours to photocopy all those bills.

ON the day of the deal, I was sitting on a rocking chair in Sears, with a duffle bag full of money. As I sat there, watching people walk by, I kept thinking, "If they only knew I was sitting here with a quarter of a million dollars!" It was so exciting.

As it turned out, after all that fuss, I didn't even have to show anyone the money. The dealer showed up with the drugs and was taken down. It was a bit anticlimactic but still fun. It was the biggest drug seizure I had ever seen.

DURING this time, I also worked a Joint Forces operation with the Niagara Regional Police Service. Their members would rotate in and out of the Drug Section every two years, so there was always a turnover of staff.

One member who was transferred from Niagara Police made highly inappropriate comments about women to me on several occasions.

Once, I'd been invited to a Drug Section party at a member's house and excused myself to use the washroom. The Niagara officer followed me right into the bathroom, grabbed me and tried to kiss me. I had to fight him off and tell him to leave me alone.

That was the end of the party for me.

I left and drove to my apartment. But just before I entered the back door to the apartment building, I was grabbed from behind and pushed up against the wall. I hadn't been aware that he'd followed me home.

He tried to kiss me again and once again I was able to fight him off as he'd had too much alcohol and was unsteady on his feet.

I never attended any future parties that were held at private residences since I felt too much at risk of being assaulted. Just when I was feeling safe, now I had two male members that I had to constantly watch out for.

After that incident, I would drive around in circles to make sure he hadn't followed me home, but now he knew where I lived. I had to more vigilant when arriving home to make sure he wasn't waiting for me.

I didn't report this incident to the RCMP as they had not taken any action in the past, but also because it involved another police agency. Within a few months, though, this member was removed from the Drug Section when complaints were made against him.

Many times during our night shifts, the guys would decide that they wanted to go for drinks at the strip clubs. I would either return to the detachment alone or go home. On more than one occasion, I would be told, "Paulette, it's time for you to go," when they were intending on going.

One of these members was a heavy drinker and had also been an undercover police officer. One day, he called the three junior members including me into the sergeant's office. He told us to take out our notebooks and to write down that we had tried to buy drugs to cover for the fact that they had gone drinking instead. He also told us to write off our files[9] so that it looked like we'd done work.

*

A few of our new members got themselves in trouble for drinking. One member had a habit of passing out in the bathroom. There was one night when everyone thought he had gone home, when in fact he was sleeping it off on the bathroom floor.

Another member, after a night of drinking, drove to a target's house in an unmarked police car, spoke to the target, then left. At that point, he decided he wasn't in any shape to drive home, but he'd left the police car running with the car door open. When the target went outside and saw

9   Conclude the files

the member's gun sitting on the front seat of the car, the Niagara Police were called. Police searched for the member, concerned that something had happened to him, but it turned out that he'd called his roommate to come pick him up and he was home sleeping it off.

ONE day, two members of the Niagara Regional Police Service and I had to travel to Headquarters in Toronto to get an Operational plan (also known as an Investigational plan) approved and while there I gave them a tour of the facility. During the tour, we stopped at the RCMP Mess and had a beverage. An RCMP officer, who had been drinking quite a bit, made a very inappropriate comment to me, unzipped his fly and pulled out his penis.

One of the Niagara members grabbed him and pulled him away from me. Other members came and pulled the RCMP officer away and we left the Mess immediately as the Niagara officers were very upset.

To my knowledge, I don't know if the Niagara officers ever told their boss or mine about the incident. I didn't, since I knew nothing would come of it and I didn't want to put our working relationship between the Niagara Regional Police and RCMP in jeopardy.

*

ONE morning, the Drug Section went out for breakfast at a restaurant near Niagara Falls that was a known hangout for the Niagara Regional Police. On our way into the restaurant, a man started taking pictures of me. I'd seen him in court before as I had testified in drug cases. He was well known to the Niagara officers for trying to get pictures of officers to sell to the motorcycles gangs. In fact, the Outlaws will pay money for pictures of undercover police officers. This was the first time I became aware of the need to keep a low profile and avoid unwanted exposure.

The guys from my section grabbed the man and took his camera away from him. After removing the 35 mm film, they returned the camera to him. This was thankfully before the days of cell phones and social media.

Chapter Fifteen

🍁

DURING THE SUMMER OF 1988, I was sent to work security at the G7 Summit. This was my first big security event, requiring me to work twelve hours shifts from 7:00 pm to 7:00 am for the duration of the summit.

I was assigned to work the security gate to the Media Square and I would let the media personnel with accredited identification enter the security tent, place their belongings into the X-ray scanner, then direct the person to walk through the personal scanner. If they set off the alarm, I would take a wand and search them for any object that might have set off the scanner.

ONE day, a gentleman had set off the scanner. I asked him to empty his pockets. He asked me if he could just tell me what he had in his pocket.

"You must empty your pockets," I repeated.

"I have condoms in my pocket," he whispered.

"That it doesn't matter, you must empty his pockets."

He took out a bundle of condoms and placed them in the basket. I scanned him with the wand. All clear.

Every night he and I went through the exact same process. He never wanted to take out his condoms. All I could think about was where in the world was he planning on using them. It was an open-air venue. No tents, no place to hide. We played this game for a week.

*

ONE of the highlights of working at the Media Square was seeing some of the TV news reporters that I had watched growing up. Surprisingly, Lloyd Robinson was as short as I was.

One of the shocking things I observed, though, were the homeless people who seemed to appear out of nowhere around 3:00 am and look into dumpsters, hoping for something to eat. I'd never seen anything like that in my life. It left a deep impression on me. I would always have a soft spot in my heart for the homeless. Although I grew up poor, I was grateful that I had not ended up like these people.

THINGS at work were good during this time and I was settling in and feeling more accepted by the members. I was even asked to stay at their homes when they went away on holidays, including the perfume wife and the wife who didn't want me to come to her home. In time, these two wives apologized to me for not trusting me to work with their husbands.

By now, two more of female members had been posted to Niagara and it felt as though things were starting to change. My supervisor, who worked for the Niagara Regional Police Service, was the best supervisor I ever had. He invited our team to his home where I met his wife and kids, and his attitude was more like that of the police I had grown up knowing in New Brunswick. He is still one of my favourite people in this world. The Niagara Police had a different mentality than the RCMP officers.

JUST as I was starting to feel like I belonged, I would soon start my life on the road. At one point, I'd asked my friend, Cathy to keep an eye out for me. I told her to pretend that I had a rope tied around my waist. If she started to see me change as a result of my undercover work, I would need her to pull on the rope to pull me back! In theory this was a great idea, but in reality, a very difficult task.

EVENTUALLY, it was decided that I could no longer buy drugs. I was apparently untrained and would not be able to continue as an undercover officer until I was properly trained on the Undercover Operators course. As a result, I was sent to be interviewed by officers from the drug program located at the RCMP headquarters in Toronto, to see if I was a suitable candidate for the course.

I drove to Toronto for the interview, and there were about fifteen other possible candidates, four of whom were my troop mates. One of my troop mates went first. She was back out within a few minutes. When I asked what happened, she said they recommended she defer for a couple of years.

When it was my turn to be interviewed the instructor stated, "You are very junior in service. I recommend you defer yourself for a couple more years. By then you will have more experience".

"No," I replied. "If I don't have it skills by now I never will".

It turned out that this was a test to see if I was confident enough in myself to go forward. It appeared that I was. The troop mates who'd deferred themselves did not get into the program.

Our interview continued and at the end I was advised that I would proceed to the second round. I would be required to take a psychological test and then, if I were successful, the members from the National headquarters in Ottawa would interview me.

I later attended the second interview and at the end of the interview, I was told I was a successful candidate and would be sent for training in British Columbia.

This would be the second time I would fly on an airplane, and this time I was bumped to First Class. It was the first and the last time I flew First Class, but it was a thrill. I could see the Rocky Mountains as we flew west—they were incredible—and I took lots of pictures. I remember flying over an area that looked the same as that of *The Beachcombers*—I could see the logs floating in the water. I had never been here before. They had green grass in November. I had never seen that before either. What a beautiful province!

I attended the Undercover Operators course in Vancouver. This was my first course, after Depot, with the RCMP. It was an amazing course and I learned so much. As an Undercover Operator, they taught us three important questions to ask: 1) How much is it? 2) Is it any good? 3) Can I get more of it? These are the three questions you need to ask when buying dope.

So that day, I was asked to go out and buy condoms using these three questions. The first question was easy. The price was marked on the box of condoms. The second question was fun. So I had to ask the pharmacist if the condoms were any good. Of course, I told him they were for a wedding shower and that I wanted to blow them up and use them as balloons. Would they burst when I tried to blow them up? I think he was more embarrassed then I was. And the third question was easy since they had a shelf full of condoms.

One of the most humbling things I had to do as part of the course was to beg for money. I used the story that my boyfriend had thrown me out and that I needed money to get home. My story wasn't working and I wasn't getting anywhere. I came across as a street person asking for money. I can't tell you how bad I felt and how badly people can treat you. People yell things at you like "Get a job" or just try hard to avoid you.

When I changed my story and told people that I'd just been mugged and my purse had been stolen, people started to give me money. I saw people with nothing giving the most or giving what they had. It was a lesson I'll keep for the rest of my life. To this day, I have a hard time seeing street people asking for money. I can't walk by without giving them something.

AS part of the course, I was encouraged to touch drugs, to feel them. Did you know that if you rub a small amount of cocaine between your fingers that it feels oily? Cocaine is cooked in kerosene! Do you know why in movies, you see the drug dealer open the package of cocaine and taste it, or rub it on his gums? Because cocaine numbs your tongue or gums! Did you know Novocain is a derivative of cocaine? That's what dentists use to freeze your gums, except it doesn't make you high. Did you know that heroin when rubbed between your fingers is sticky? It's sugar based and that's why most heroin addicts crave sugar and have rotten teeth, due to their high consumption of sugar.

ON one occasion, I was sent into a gay bar where I approached a man and bought a gram of cocaine for $100. After the deal the man said, "Use it on tissue." I thanked him and assured him that I would, but in my mind, I wondered what the heck that meant.

The next day, I described my transaction in front of the class and asked if anyone knew what the tissue thing was all about. It turns out, you put the cocaine on bathroom tissue and wiped it up your bum! Yuck. The things you learn.

In the course, they also asked us to handle syringes, and I was asked to insert a needle into my vein. Luckily, I am not afraid of needles, but one of the guys seeing a needle, sounded like he was going to throw up and ran out of the room. I placed my belt around my left bicep and pulled it tight with my teeth. I got the syringe ready, then picked it up with my right hand. Surprisingly, my hand was steady as I picked up the needle and inserted it into my puffed-up vein. I felt the cold steel tip enter my vein. It felt like a little bee sting.

AT the end of the course, each candidate would be told whether or not they were successful. If you were successful, you'd be told whether you could do short-term or long-term jobs and whether you were best suited for soft drugs (such as marihuana or hash) or hard drugs (such as cocaine or heroin). I was told I'd passed the course successfully and was suitable for long term and hard drugs.

To celebrate the end of the course, like most courses, we had a party. We went out to a pub owned by the Irish Rovers. One of the members asked the waitress to bring him three raw eggs and three wine glasses. He told us that he was going to challenge two of us to do what he was going to show us. He cracked the egg and poured it into the wine glass. He then took the glass containing the raw egg and placed it under his nose. Lastly, he snorted the egg up his nose then swallowed it. That was gross.

When he asked for two volunteers, one guy agreed. He cracked open the egg and placed it in the wine glass, put the glass under his nose and snorted the egg, but this time the yoke broke. Half the yoke was in his throat and the other half hanging from his nose. The more he tried to snort the rest of the yoke up, the messier it got. It was very gross and very funny, but there was no way I was going to do that. Believe me when I say they tried to make me.

So, because I wouldn't try snorting the egg, they took my brand-new Hush Puppy shoe off my foot and poured beer in it, then passed it around so that everyone could drink from it. I never got that beer stain out of my shoe! These guys knew how to drink.

Chapter Sixteen

🍁

AFTER THE THREE-WEEK COURSE, I returned to Niagara, and within a few days I was given my undercover identification number. This was the only way you could be identified so that your name would not be used in reports and to try to protect your true identity should these documents get disclosed to the public.

Shortly after that, I was sent to London, Ontario for my first undercover job as a trained UCO. For the first month, I lived in a hotel room. During this undercover operation, I would be wearing a wire as a one-way transmitting device. This would allow the cover team to stay outside of the bars, and still hear my conversations. It was also used as a security device in case I needed help. Knowing that every time I had to use the bathroom the guys could hear every sound I made, I used to whistle so they wouldn't know.

THE first time I walked into the Talbot Inn and sat by the bar, the TV right in front of me lost its signal. I then heard a patron at the bar comment that the cops must be around. Shocked by this, I reached into my purse and turned the transmitter off. The TV signal came back on. Note to self: Don't sit too close to the TV. Once again, it was learn as you go. No one had bothered to tell me that would happen.

At a later time when I was working that bar, I'd gone into the women's washroom and some girls were doing lines of cocaine of the counter. Another woman was standing there with a switchblade in her hands just flicking the switchblade open and closed over and over again. That gives you a sense of the type of atmosphere in which I worked every day.

*

AFTER the first month, I was moved into a house. I worked straight night shifts from 4:00 pm to midnight for three months and stayed at the safe house during most weekends. I slept in the upstairs bedroom.

One weekend, I went home and upon my return, I noticed that the windows in my bedroom had been sealed up with cardboard. I thought that was great as there was light from the streetlights coming in at night. I had mentioned that to the team, so I thought they'd solved that problem for me.

Then I noticed that the bed had clean sheets on it. I thought it was weird that the guys would change my bedding. One of the members, Joe admitted he had changed them, but I found out eventually that the darkened windows and clean sheets were not intended for my benefit at all. He was having an affair with the house owner and was using the safe house to meet her when I wasn't there. It seems, this was common knowledge. At the time, I thought it was disgusting that someone was sleeping in the same bed that I was expected to sleep in.

ONE night, Joe arrived at the safe house and asked me to go for a drive. I was thrilled to get out of the house since I was going stir crazy. He told me we were going to visit a mutual friend who lived in Stratford. I was excited to see her as I hadn't seen her since Depot.

When we arrived, I was surprised to see two of my friends here. Next thing I know Joe and the second friend were hugging and kissing and acting like a couple. On the way home, he explained that he was dating my friend. It turns out they'd met while he was doing an undercover job.

He requested that should his wife ever call the safe house, I should tell her that he'd just left. I wondered how his wife would even know the safe house number. So there he was, dating the homeowner and my friend and he had a wife. What a busy man.

I later found out that this member was also dating a police officer from Woodstock. I had met his wife and his two beautiful daughters, and I felt so bad for her and the kids. I couldn't believe he was cheating on her, and I was upset at being put in that position where he expected me to lie for him.

ANOTHER night, while working at Pub McCann's, I tied to buy cocaine from a waitress. She said that she would sell me cocaine if I did a line of cocaine in front of her. I told her I didn't snort cocaine, I mainlined it.[10] She asked me to follow her to the bathroom, then opened a stall and asked me to get in with her. Asking to see my track marks, I rolled up my sleeve and showed her my needle mark, the same ones I had learned how to do on the undercover course. Then she asked me to inject it in front of her, but I told her I couldn't because sometimes I threw up when I injected cocaine so I couldn't do it there.

She finally believed me and sold me one gram of cocaine for $100. It took a lot of effort to buy drugs because the smart drug dealers were always testing you to make sure you weren't a cop. I'd learned that coke users could vomit after using coke, as earlier during this project I had driven a guy to get us cocaine. He did his coke in the car, but soon yelled at me to stop. As I stopped the car, he opened the door and threw up. This gave me another

---

10   Injected it

excuse I could use so that I didn't have to use drugs.

*

DURING this undercover job, I had to use my own money to purchase my meals and beverages since the cover man didn't provide me with any funds except the money to buy drugs. That had never happened in Niagara. This became very expensive for me as all of these meals and beverages were bought in pubs and bars. At last, feeling I could no longer afford to subsidize this work, I asked to be sent home.

When the NCO in charge of the Drug Section called me in to ask me why, I advised him of my money issue. He asked me why I hadn't put in my expense claims. I told him what I'd been told by my cover man and it turned out the cover man had been putting my expense money into his own personal bank account. Because of this, my expense claims were paid and I was able to stay and finished the job.

ONCE and only once, during the London undercover job, I fronted my money to a guy who said he would sell me drugs. I gave him $50 for half a gram of coke. "Wait here," he told me. "I'll be right back."

I waited and waited. Finally, it hit me that he had ripped me off. I was so embarrassed when I had to tell my cover team that I had just given away $50.

DURING another drug purchase, the suspect asked me for the money and told me that he would go and get the dope. Having been "once bitten", I said "No".

He assured me that he wouldn't rip me off. Famous last words, right? So I asked him for his wallet to hold while he went to get the drugs.

He agreed.

After he stepped out of the car, I opened his wallet and found it contained a hundred dollars, his credit cards and ID. After he returned, he handed me the drugs and left. I was getting smarter. I never ever fronted money again for the rest of my undercover days.

FOR me, one of the toughest parts of the London UCO job was when I was buying hash oil from a couple with two very young kids, about two and three years of age. The parents would cook the hash oil in the kitchen of their apartment and sell it right in front of the kids.

One night I arrived at the apartment to buy some drugs and found the two kids sitting at the door crying. The apartment door was open. At first, I thought that something had happened to the parents. I didn't see any blood and couldn't find the parents so I took the kids in my arms and tried to comfort them.

About 20 minutes later, the mother arrived carrying a twenty-four case of beer. She claimed that she'd had a fight with her boyfriend and had gone to the Beer Store to get him some beer for when he came home. She claimed she'd only been gone a few minutes.

I felt guilty knowing that both parents would be arrested and I worried about the children. When I had to go to court to testify against the parents for trafficking drugs, they brought their kids to court with them. Once the kids saw me, they tried to run to me, but their mother and father held them back and told them I was bad because I was trying to take their parents away from them. That was devastating to hear.

There were times that I liked the people who sold me drugs. They weren't bad people, but they were selling drugs and I worried that maybe I wasn't cut out for undercover work if I felt bad about what I was doing.

THE project ended in February 1989 and, of course, there was a party to celebrate. A member of the cover team told me that the guys might have something planned for me at the party, so I figured I had better plan something myself. I went shopping and brought a few gifts of my own.

During the party, the sergeant in charge read a prepared speech. It spoke about how I had done such a great job, how I had lost some money but that I still hadn't lost my virginity. So then it was my turn.

I pulled out a key chain with 20 keys on it and told them I was returning all their house keys. Then I held up a large pair of tiger-striped men's underwear and handed it to the guy in charge of the project. Then I reached into my bag and pulled out the largest pair of women's underwear I could find, held them up and said, "All I want to know is who in the world do these belong to?" I had the last laugh!

ULTIMATELY as a result of that job, a total of twenty-five people were arrested and over 100 charges laid. At the end of the project, the cover team presented me with a plaque. On the back one person written, "You don't pull on Superman's cape, you don't spit into the wind, you don't pull the mask off the Lone Ranger and you don't front your own money!" Another lesson learned the hard way.

AFTER the Undercover job in London was finished, I was contacted by internal affairs and was questioned about my whereabouts on certain dates. I reviewed my notebooks for each date in question and I'd been working undercover in Windsor.

The cover man in London had been caught using the RCMP credit card to pay for personal trips to visit his girlfriend and had used me as his alibi. I couldn't believe that he had used me to try to cover for his activities. This was a member who was responsible for my health and safety.

As it turned out, he was dating a person he'd arrested for trafficking drugs. It was of great concern to me as I didn't know if he'd exposed me, my name or my photo to this person and if I could be at risk for future undercover jobs. Once again, I felt betrayed and angry. Sadly, the investigation against this member was poorly done and he kept his job working for the RCMP.

AFTER an undercover operator completes an undercover project, they are required by policy to be assessed by a psychiatrist. I attended my mandatory appointment and met with the doctor. He spoke to me for about five minutes. Never asked me how I was, how I had been treated, whether or not I had any issues. Nothing. He told me to write an exam, which took about an hour and a half to complete. Then I was gone.

I would do this again and again with the same doctor for years. Never any questions. Just write the test and go. It would take years before I met with another doctor who asked me questions the first doctor never had, but by then it was way too late. The burnout of working undercover was starting to take its toll.

Chapter Seventeen

✦

IMMEDIATELY AFTER THE UNDERCOVER JOB in London ended, I was sent to Windsor in April 1989 to do another undercover job, this time living in an apartment. It was another street level drug job, going into bars and trying to buy as much dope as I could. My cover team was made up of four guys, three of them RCMP officers and one from the Windsor Police. Two of the Mounties were undercover officers just like me.

It was another three month of night shifts, eating and drinking and buying dope.

Once again, I worked a shift of 4:00 pm to midnight. On many nights, I was lucky to have three people covering me, but most nights it was only two.

Eventually, I was brought into the detachment to meet the Drug Section commander, and he asked how things were going. I told him that I wasn't happy about the lack of coverage. At times, I would go out to make a drug purchase with only two people there to cover me and I felt I was being put at unnecessary risk. He seemed surprised when I told him that the supervisor had never come out when I was working, and that another member was always late or not working at all. The next thing I knew four more members were assigned to the team. The supervisor apologized and we got on with the business of buying drugs.

HAVING two other members who were also undercover officers turned out to be a mixed blessing. My cover team threw eggs at a neighbouring apartment across the street one night because they thought it was funny, but I felt badly as I watched the man who had to clean it up. Yet another night, they decided we needed to have fun and hosted a party at the house of one of the cover team members. They constantly wanted to have fun by attending parties, drinking, and going out to eat, to the point where I believed that they didn't care if I actually made any drug purchases.

I felt frustrated and yet I was relieved to have a break. I'd been buying drugs for well over a year and was starting to feel burned out. I knew something was wrong. I asked for a week off and they agreed. I went home to see my parents for the week and returned feeling better and ready to get back to work. Or so I thought.

USUALLY once I had made a drug buy, I would return to the safe house, write my notes and turn over the drugs to the cover team. I'd write detailed notes about the purchase and include a description of the person whom I had bought the drugs from to help the cover team identify the suspect.

One night, while sitting in a bar, I bought a gram of cocaine from a guy and he began hitting on me and told me he wanted to perform oral sex on me. He told me he used to have a long moustache, pulling out his driver's license to show me his picture. While he was admiring his moustache, I was admiring his personal information.

I excused myself to go to the bathroom and once there I wrote the man's name, date of birth and address on bathroom tissue paper and stuffed it in my purse. You can imagine the surprise of my cover team when I was able to tell them these details. This would be the easiest identification ever.

Later during the trial, his lawyer asked me how I had got the accused to show me his driver's licence. I skipped the oral sex part and told the judge he'd wanted to show me what he looked like when he had a longer moustache.

At the end of the project, the police brought each person I had purchased drugs from into a room where I was sitting and they were asked if they knew me. One person in particular, stood up for me and said, "Paulette is my friend she doesn't do drugs."

When I received a signal, I identified myself to her as a police officer and held up my badge. She fainted. When she came to, she was extremely upset and they had to restrain her as she lunged at me. I had a strange way of making enemies.

The project ended in July 1989 with the arrests of fourteen, the seizure of weapons including a handgun and approximately $15,000 worth of narcotics.

AT the end of the undercover job in Windsor, I returned to my regular Drug Section duties in Niagara Detachment. On my first day back, a member told me that he'd had to look after my files while I was having fun.

Fun?

Working undercover is far from fun. You have to be on your game every single night. Who is selling drugs? Is anyone watching me? Can I buy drugs from another dealer in the same bar without getting caught? Remember the details of each drug buy so that I can record them in my notes and help to get a conviction in court. Are there any weapons or other added risks? What excuse will I need to use so that they don't pressure me to drink or use drugs? Try to buy drugs from each dealer at least twice to show the courts that it actually was a dealer and not just a person doing you a favour. Did you see them deal drugs to other people? Did they have more drugs on them?

Aside from these obvious stresses, another problem with working undercover is that you can't be seen with your cover team. Therefore, you have to spend a lot of time by yourself. You wait in the apartment all day until the team arrives, gives you money to buy drugs, tells you which bars they want you to go to, then you're off to work trying to buy dope. Alone.

When you are working undercover you get lonely. You look forward to going out just to have someone to talk to. At one point, I'd decided to drive back to Niagara and pick up my cat just for company. At least I would have my cat to spend my time with.

I was glad to see this particular undercover job come to an end. Not my idea of fun!

Chapter Eighteen

🍁

FROM 1989 TO 1990 I worked my shifts in Niagara. I also continued to work undercover buying drugs and travelled back and forth for court dates in London and Windsor, driving back and forth alone. Because I'd purchased drugs from a large number of people and they could cause me harm, I had to stay in hotels and eat in the hotel or in restaurants with other officers as it was no longer safe for me to be alone in those cities.

ONE night in Niagara, we were preparing to attend a townhouse to execute a search warrant. Since we'd previously executed a warrant at this residence, we knew we had to conduct a forceful entry. This was where, on our last visit, the suspect pulled out a shotgun and pointed his weapon at us while his girlfriend tried to flush the drugs down the toilet.

We met to discuss how we would gain entry on this occasion. The suspect had a steel door and a forced entry would be difficult. My thoughts were, *Use your imagination, deliver flowers, food, there are a number of reasons people knock on the door. It may even be another person looking to score drugs.*

I ended up suggesting that we get a pizza box and pretend to make a pizza delivery in order to get the front door open. Having got an empty pizza box and returned to the team, I asked who would be going to the door.

No one volunteered.

I suggested it would involve going to the door, announcing that their pizza order had arrived, and when the suspect said they had not ordered a pizza, asking them to sign the receipt to verify that they had not ordered it. That way the suspect would open the steel door and we could get in. I said that it would be better for a guy to do this part of the job as most delivery people were men.

Still no one would volunteer to do it.

In frustration, I grabbed the box, went to the door and played out the scenario until the suspect opened the door and I followed him into the kitchen. As I walked into the kitchen, a drug deal was in the process of being completed. Then the rest of the team entered the residence and arrested all the people inside.

At a time when many officers were resentful of the fact that women were entering their profession, once again I had been the first one in the door and put at the highest risk of getting hurt or injured. I was getting tired of always being the first one into a dangerous situation and felt they were taking advantage of me

ANOTHER night we were going through some Crime Stoppers reports. We had received a report that the person in question was a drug dealer and sold drugs to the strippers. We didn't have any "buy money", so I was asked to go and meet the suspect, and once I saw the cocaine, leave the coffee shop and say I was going to get the money and be right back. Then I would meet up with the cover team and go back and arrest him.

I shouldn't have gone out without proper cover, but things happened so quickly that we just acted on it.

I was dropped off near the coffee shop with no radio or cell phone to contact my cover. There were only three of us, so we hopped in one car and headed to a coffee shop to make the call to the drug dealer. The team dropped me off and told me they would watch for me to come out of the coffee shop. That was the plan.

I entered the coffee shop alone and walked over to a pay phone and called the drug dealer. Using a French accent, I explained I was a stripper and was told by the other girls that I could buy some coke from him. I told him where I was—he agreed to meet me there—and that I wanted an eight ball of coke. Then I waited for him to arrive.

A few minutes later a man drove up in a Trans Am and entered the coffee shop, looking around as if searching for someone. I got up and spoke to him, still using a French accent, and he said, "Let's sit down."

When he asked to see my ID, I told him I didn't have any. Then he wanted to know who had given me his name. I gave a name, but he said he didn't know her. I said, "Well maybe she uses a stage name."

He eventually agreed to sell me the drugs for $300. I told him I only had one hundred but that I lived around the corner and would get the rest and be right back. He was very uneasy.

He asked me to go out to his car, but I refused. He then asked me to go out behind the coffee shop. I felt I had no choice so I walked out with him, hoping that my cover team would come in and arrest him. Remember, that was the plan.

We walked to the back of the coffee shop. Once there, the suspect asked me to take my top off, saying he thought I was a police agent or informant and wanted to see if l was wearing a wire. This deal was going badly and I was getting very scared, as my cover wasn't coming to my location.

I lifted my shirt to show him my waistline. I wasn't wearing a wire. He asked me to turn around. I did so but all the while keeping my eyes on him since I knew I was in a dangerous situation. He seemed to relax when he saw I wasn't wearing a wire so I started to walk away as if I were going to get the rest of the money.

As I was walking away, I saw him get in his car and follow me. I couldn't find my cover and was starting to get really scared, as I couldn't get away from him. Finally, my cover team drove toward me and I ran to the car. I let them know that the suspect was following me and was in the car just behind me. We ended up pulling over the suspect's car and arrested him for selling drugs.

The suspect was a member of the Satan's Choice motorcycle gang and he had an ounce of cocaine stuffed down the front of his pants. I was very upset that my cover hadn't helped me at the back of the coffee shop. I felt that I had once again been put into a dangerous situation and they should have been there to protect me. This time, I was actually seriously afraid for my life for the very first time.

As it turned out, within a couple of weeks the suspect was arrested and charged with first-degree murder. He could have easily taken my life that night. It was not the first time or the last that I would be put at risk due to lack of support from my team.

ANOTHER officer and I were working together in the Fort Erie area one night. This time, I had a Crime Stoppers report that a woman was selling marihuana from her house. My partner and I set up surveillance on the house, but there seemed to be no activity there so I told my partner that I would approach the house and try to make a drug purchase. I approached the residence and a woman answered the door. When I asked to buy some weed, she stated she didn't know who I was and that she didn't sell to people she didn't know.

Meeting up again with my partner, I told him what she'd said and I convinced him to go back to confront the woman and try to get her to hand over any drugs she had. We knocked on the door and identified ourselves as police officers, and I told her we had a Crime Stoppers tip that she was selling drugs. She admitted she had drugs in the house, but unfortunately we were there working by ourselves, meaning one of us would have to stay at the house while the other would have to drive back to the office, type a search warrant, get it sworn and then come back. So without talking to my partner, I told her that if she handed them over, I wouldn't charge her. She agreed.

She walked into her bedroom and came out with a green garbage bag full of marihuana, over a pound of it. I told her that if she sold more drugs, we would get another Crime Stoppers tip and the next time she would be charged and go to jail.

The next day my boss called me I into his office and asked why we had a pound of marihuana in the exhibit locker but no charges. I told him I'd given my word that if she handed over the drugs, I wouldn't charge her, and since we were only two officers, that seemed like a good deal all around. We never received any other Crime Stoppers reports on that address, so I like to think that my idea worked.

ONE day my partner and I were driving back to the detachment when we heard a member requesting help. He'd driven off the road and was in the ditch. Since we were close by, we told him we'd get to the scene and give him a hand.

We drove to the location he'd given us but couldn't find him. This member had a reputation for getting lost, so we asked him to confirm his location. He provided the same information so we drove by again. Still no luck.

We told him we were at the location, but couldn't see him so we asked him to stand by the road. Moments later we saw him. He had driven his car about twenty feet down into the ditch and so could not possibly be seen from the road.

We called a tow truck and waited for it to arrive. When it finally arrived, the tow truck driver said he needed someone to steer the car up the embankment. The member suggested, "Paulette why don't you sit in the car and stay warm and I will stand up here and block the traffic." I agreed.

The tow truck driver gave me some instructions and began to tow the car up the hill. It wasn't until I got up to the roadway that it dawned on me that all the traffic would see was a female driver sitting behind the wheel of the car that she'd obviously driven into the ditch. We laughed about that for a long time.

ON many occasions, when we were able to do a search warrant, the guys would ask me to go knock on the door, since people would more likely answer the door for a female. On one such occasion, we were about to enter a "crack house" where we knew a firearm was present.

I went to the door and a man opened the door to let me in. I followed him into the apartment and then the rest of the team made their way in, announcing that we were the police. The male suspect I'd been following turned around, reached into his pocket and pulled out a gun. Since I was the one closest to him, I jumped on him and shouted out, "Gun!"

I took him to the floor and another member came to assist me. Once he was handcuffed and the gun secured, my body started to shake. I knew I had come very close to being shot, injured or even killed.

When I had a chance at last to look around, I saw a trail of bullets from the doorway all the way to where he'd pulled his gun out. We had met them in the lobby and they probably knew we were the police so he'd been loading the gun and getting ready to use it on us. It seemed that this suspect was in the country illegally and, after he served his sentence, he was deported.

Working on another file in Welland, I approached a residence where we had previously purchased cocaine. A search warrant had been obtained and we were executing the warrant at the residence. As we entered, we yelled, "Police! Search Warrant! Everyone to get on the floor!"

They did so, but we soon realized there were more suspects than police. Luckily, I noticed one suspect reaching around his waistband and realized he was lying on top of a gun. Yet another raid and another gun.

Cocaine was seized as well as the sawed-off shotgun. Thankfully, once again no one was hurt. Three people were charged and about $3,000 of cocaine was seized.

Guns were becoming a common occurrence when conducting drug raids and around this time officers began wearing bulletproof vests. No more push back about wearing vests. It had become very dangerous to be on the Drug Squad.

GUNS were not the only danger, as soon became apparent. On one drug raid, we were told that there was a live cougar in the house. We didn't know where the animal was in the house or whether it was restrained so, as we approached, we had our guns out.

We entered the house and found the cougar in the basement, which allegedly had once belonged to a stripper who'd used the creature in her act. In fact, she owed so much money to the drug dealer that she'd handed the cougar over to him as payment. Sadly, the drug dealer, trying to look like a good citizen, had been taking the cougar to schools.

It was my job to deal with the animal. The owners put a chain and leash on him and handed it to me. I was surprised at what a strong animal he was. Although it turned out the cougar had no teeth or claws, I could barely hold on to him so we locked it up in a room. Disappointingly, in the end, the suspect was allowed to keep the cougar.

WHEN working undercover, we are taught to go in and out the same door. That way, the cover team knows where you will come out of the bar and keep an eye out for you. Only once did I break that rule, and as a result the cover team lost me. Because I had a listening device, I hoped that they'd heard me leaving the bar. I was able to make the purchase and return safely to the bar, but the cover team was very pissed off. I never made that mistake again. Another lesson learned.

THERE are times when you have a false sense of security. You know what's going on, but your cover team doesn't. This really didn't hit home until I had to cover an undercover operator. I was very nervous, worrying about their safety, because I understood exactly how they felt and knew what the dangers were.

There were times, I must admit, that I didn't care if I took chances. Maybe if I got hurt, I wouldn't have to do this anymore. No matter where I worked, everyone wanted me to work undercover. After a while I was tired of it, but I couldn't say no. I was my own worst enemy, always wanting to please others at my own peril. What had been my gold ticket of acceptance was now my noose.

*

SOON after that came a night when a member from another team asked me if I would go out to buy some drugs for them. I turned around and yelled, "No!" I just couldn't do it.

The member was in disbelief that I'd refused and asked me if I was okay. I had NEVER refused to go out and make a buy. I went home and felt so guilty that I couldn't sleep that night.

The next day I went into work and told him I was sorry and that I would go with him that day to buy the drugs. In the back of my mind, I knew I was struggling but wouldn't admit it. I just kept pushing forward.

Chapter Nineteen

❦

I ATTENDED THE DRUG AWARENESS Presenter course in January of 1990 in Toronto, which would come in handy later in my career. I took two very important lessons away from this course.

On the first day, the instructor asked us to draw a drug dealer. Our group came up with a male with long hair, a beard, black leather jacket, jeans and boots. He looked like a typical motorcycle gang member. The other groups also had rough looking men. What I learned from this is that we were stereotyping drug dealers as men who looked rough. The lesson our instructor drilled into us was that anyone could be a drug dealer. A doctor, a woman, a man in a suit and tie.

The other lesson was the Smarties test. The instructor opened up a box of Smarties and asked everyone to take one and put it on their desk. Sometime later, she told us to go ahead and eat the Smarties. We did. Shortly after that, the instructor asked us how we were feeling. She asked us if we knew her, really knew her, and we realized that we didn't actually know her very well at all. She also asked us if we knew for sure that what we'd eaten were actual Smarties.

She'd cleverly made her point. We ate it because she told us to. We took it from someone we didn't really know. And we were the police! I would use those teaching points for years.

IN September 1990, I was assigned another undercover job in Ottawa. The shifts were from 9:00 pm to 5:00 am and this assignment was for four months. Myself and another female undercover officer were living in a hotel suite in Ottawa.

At first, the cleaning staff would wake us up by knocking on our door, as they wanted to clean our room. So that we could get some sleep, we had to make arrangements with the hotel not to clean our room until later, agreeing to leave our room at noon each day to allow the staff to clean it.

Once again, we ate all our meals in restaurants and consumed alcohol when we were working in bars. At least we had each other to talk to, but we both felt isolated and lonely.

THERE was a lot of violence during this UCO job. There was a drug war going on between groups who wanted to control the drug trade, and we observed fights, stabbing and were personally threatened. One of the suspects we hung around with was even threatened right in front of us when a man took a knife to her throat and said he was going to kill her. As we approached her, he backed down and left. And as always, there was also the constant threat of exposure.

One night, while working in one of the bars, I was greeted by an RCMP officer I knew, who was in Ottawa attending a training course. I told him I was working and to pretend he didn't know me. Luckily, none of the targets saw this.

Another night, I was waiting in a line to buy coke—there were at least three other people lined up in front of me. I saw the suspect reach into a clear plastic bag, take out a deck of cocaine and give it to the person who then paid him money. Then the next person, and the next, then me. That night, I wrote up my notes detailing that I had seen the drug dealer sell coke to three other people before I made my purchase.

Much later, during his court case, the Crown laid an additional three trafficking charges and possession for the purpose of trafficking based on my notes. He was convicted of all charges and the Crown thanked me for my detailed notes, which resulted in the four extra charges against the accused.

Sadly, another suspect I'd purchased drugs from was on the Canadian Olympic boxing team and when it came time to arrest him, he resisted arrest and had to be taken down at gunpoint.

The project ended in November with our having arrested twenty-eight suspects and over fifty charges being laid.

AFTER this job, I returned once again to my duties in Niagara, but in the spring of 1991, I was assigned another undercover job in Sudbury and Elliott Lake, working with an agent. This particular agent had a cocaine addiction andhad agreed to help the police by turning in his cocaine supplier. My job was to work with him on this.

I would work on shift in Niagara, then take the RCMP plane to Sudbury, rent a car and drive two hours to Elliott Lake. I'd stay in a hotel for two or three days, then drive back to Sudbury and take the RCMP plane back to Niagara.

ONE time, while flying up to Sudbury, the plane had to land at Buttonville Airport. The tower told the pilot he was fourth for landing. The pilot initially counted two planes in front of him. So once again, the pilot looked around and still counted two planes. Then he said to me, "We must be number three for landing."

We watched the first plane land, then the second. As the pilot was getting ready to land, he looked around one last time for another plane. It was only then, as the plane started to descend, that we saw we were flying directly on top of the third plane. The pilot pulled up and we got quickly out of the way. If I hadn't seen the look on the pilot's face, I would have thought he was playing a joke on me, but clearly this had been no joke.

THE target of this job was a serious threat and it became clear that there were not enough people assigned to cover me. During our conversations the target told me about his drug transportation routes from Quebec to northern Ontario. He even bragged abou the time he blew up an OPP[11] cruiser.

ONE night, he showed up with an open bottle of alcohol. I guess he thought he was going to stay for a while and have a few drinks. Like that was going to happen.

I don't remember what I said to him, but I made it clear that I had something better to do. I told him I wanted to buy an ounce of cocaine.

By the end of the project, the target was arrested and charged. Once he found out that I was a police officer, he took a contract out on my life. He hired two men and sent them to where he thought I was staying and told them to "get Paulette".

I was called by the member in charge of the file and told to stay low and keep an eye out. Having told me he was behind the bombing of an OPP cruiser, I knew what the targert was capable of.

WHILE I was doing the undercover job, I had very long curly hair and when we met with his lawyer, he explained that he was going to use the femme fatale defence, saying that he was attracted to me which is why he told me everything—he was going to say that he had made it up because he was trying to impress me. Knowing this, when I showed up for the trial, I

---

11   Ontario Provincial Police

cut m hair very short. So when I appeared in court with virtually no hair, his defense changed quickly to, "I was drunk!"

*

I did this job for about two months straight, working weekends in Elliot Lake, and between these trips, still going back and forth to court in London, Windsor, Ottawa and later Sault Ste. Marie, as well as working my regular job in Niagara. On more than one occasion while working with this agent, he acted as if he were high on drugs and coming down off them, having seizures in the car.

I ultimately walked off this job and refused to continue to work with him because I feared for my safety. I knew the agent was not trustworthy. Thankfully, when I brought forward my concerns this time, the agent was removed, and I was ordered not to return to this UCO job by the Commanding Officer.

WHILE I was doing the undercover job, I had very long curly hair and when we met with his lawyer, he explained that he was going to use the femme fatale defence, saying that he was attracted to me which is why he told me everything—he was going to say that he had made it up because he was trying to impress me. Knowing this, when I showed up for the trial, I cut my hair very short. So when I appeared in court with very little hair, looking almost masculine, his defence changed quickly to, "I was drunk!"

Chapter Twenty

🍁

AFTER THE JOB IN THE North, my boss assigned me to do drug lectures. It was a great opportunity for me to unwind from my undercover jobs and a chance to educate children, parents and interested groups about the dangers of drugs.

I loved talking about drugs. I had learned so much by buying drugs that now I could share that knowledge with others. And the more I lectured, the more requests would come in. I looked forward to the next and the next and the next lecture. For well over a year, I was lecturing full time and enjoying every minute of it.

One example of what I was able to tell parents was this: each September at the beginning of the school year, the rumour mill starts spinning the story about kids in school being given LSD in the form of stickers. We got a lot of calls from concerned parents about this. The truth is, drug dealers don't give their drugs away for free, so it's very unlikely that this could happen. In my thirty years of service, I'd NEVER heard of one case where this has happened, but it helps to bring awareness to the parents and kids.

Another thing that amazes me is that people believe everything they see on TV. They believe that whatever a cop does on TV, the real cops can do too. For instance, we had one drug dealer who would cover his mouth every time he spoke to someone. He honestly believed that we could read his lips. After all, they can on TV!

I was also asked during this time to prepare a lecture for the Niagara Regional Police. We would identify suspected drug dealers in each area of the region and present this to the front-line police officers. I prepared a handout with pictures of the suspects, last known address, type of Narcotic being sold and how to handle these drugs. Inside the handout were the contact numbers of each member of the drug section. I advised that the drug section was available to provide assistance at any time. By training these officers on the local drug dealers in their areas, it brought awareness to the front line officers to the targets the drug section were investigating. Through doing this, I found I really developed a passion for training other officers.

*

AS always, however, there was the usual ongoing work to be done on a daily basis. On one drug file, the suspected drug dealer lived on the Niagara Parkway, his house facing the Niagara River. It was hard to do surveillance on this house as traffic was always moving and there were no spots to park a car that enabled us to keep an eye on the house. Then someone came up with the idea of renting a boat and doing surveillance from the boat.

One of the members owned a boat and loaned it to the Drug Section, so two Niagara officers and myself set out to do the surveillance. We'd bring some binoculars, a camera and some fishing poles to make it look like we were just fishing. We hooked up the trailer and were ready to set out. Next thing I know we are stopping at the Beer Store. The one officer said we could only *really* look like we were fishing if we had beer. So after the purchase of beer and ice, we were on our way.

We got in the boat and set the anchor in the river just across from the suspect's house. Fishing rods in hand, camera ready and cold beer. One of the Niagara officers took the pictures while we sat out there for hours. Back then we used cameras with 35 mm film. No cell phones, no digital cameras, just old-fashioned film.

Sometime later I took the film from the camera and waited to get the pictures developed. I was told that the film must be sent to the forensic section in Ottawa for processing so I packed it up and sent it to Ottawa.

A few weeks later, I got called into the boss's office. He wasn't happy. Handing me the pictures from the surveillance we had done on the boat, he asked if there was anything wrong with the pictures. I looked through them and didn't see any issues. I said, "They look all right to me."

He then told me that the next time I do surveillance not to take pictures of us drinking beer and ask the forensic section to process them. He didn't tell us not to drink on duty, just not to take pictures of it!

Chapter Twenty-One

🍁

ON ONE OCCASION, I WAS seconded to work at Cornwall Detachment because they needed additional security at the border. The border was situated between Cornwall, the United States and the Native reserve. I was assigned to work at the border for one month.

During a night shift, a car was re-entering Canada and instead of rolling down his window, the driver held his badge up to the window then drove away. I could have called in a "running of the port", but instead I recorded his badge number and reported him to his police service. I later found out that he'd also been seconded to the border for security, and didn't feel he needed to stop because he had nothing to declare. I told his supervisor that he more than anyone knew better than to do that.

That officer was relieved of his border duties and sent back to his detachment. I hated it when people used their positions to try to get away with something. Police should be the first people to follow the rules just like everyone else.

DURING the Gulf War in Iraq from 1991 to 1992, Toronto International Airport increased security by seconding more members to work there. As a result, I myself was seconded to Toronto Airport for three months.

These were twelve-hour shifts from 7:00 am to 7:00 pm for the first two shifts, and then it switched to 7:00 pm to 7:00 am on the last two shifts. I was living in a hotel close to the airport during this time, and at the end of our four-days of shifts, it was expected that we would return to Niagara during our four days off to save money on hotels and meals. This often resulted in us driving after being awake for more than fourteen hours.

During one night-shift, a member was involved with an irrational male passenger, who was being denied boarding his flight and he called for backup over the radio. Responding that I was on my way to assist, he insisted over the radio that he wanted a male to back him up. I went to the scene anyway and defused the situation, but the damage had been done.

I'd worked with this member for two or three years in Niagara Drug section. It wasn't that he didn't know me or what I was capable of, but the fact that when he was stressed and asking for help, he made the announcement over the radio system, for all members to hear that he didn't want a female backup. Other females on the watch later approached me to talk about the fact that the males often didn't want a female backup.

We still had a long way to go to gain acceptance by the men in the RCMP. Not everyone was like that, but it did exist and happened more than it should. Years later, this officer would apologize to me.

UPON my return to Niagara, I went back to buying drugs. In December 1991, I was working undercover in St. Catharines. I was dropped off near the bus terminal and walked around for a little bit, trying to look like I was waiting for a bus, and watched. I spotted one man dealing marihuana.

Waiting for him to finish making a drug deal, I then asked him how much for a gram. His price was ten dollars, so I took ten dollars out of my pocket and handed it to him. Then he handed me a gram of marihuana wrapped in clear plastic wrap and I stuck it in my right front pants pocket.

I also saw a man selling crack cocaine. I observed him holding out a small handful of white chucks wrapped in plastic. When I asked him how much, he stated $20 for a small and $50 for a large rock. So I took out fifty dollars and looked for the largest rock, placing that buy in my left front pants pocket as he took my money.

Having left the bus terminal, I walked over to where my cover team was parked, and as I was giving them the descriptions of the two suspects, I noticed that the man who'd sold me the crack cocaine was walking toward us. While I was opening the door of the vehicle to get out and arrest him, he took one look at me and started to run. I took off after him and one of my cover men came too. The other cover man stayed in the vehicle.

As I was chasing the suspect, he kept looking back toward me. I yelled at him to stop. I couldn't figure out why he was running away so I yelled, "Police! Stop!" He still kept running.

At some point, I ran past the Niagara Regional Police Headquarters building. I looked to see if any of their officers were in the parking lot. No such luck. It was then that I decided to yell, "Police! Stop or I'll shoot!"

I didn't actually have a gun, but what did he know? To make my case stronger yet, I raised my arm and pointed my finger at him as if I were holding a gun. So there I was, running after the suspect, pointing my finger at him like it was a gun. But all that did was make him run faster.

I yelled at him again, "You'd better be a marathon runner because I'm going to catch you". He just kept running and glancing back.

He turned down a main street and kept running. By this point, I had no idea where my cover team was and I was starting to get winded from running. As luck would have it, it was garbage night and people had put their garbage out to the curb. When the suspect turned around again to see where I was, he ran into a Lazy Boy chair that had been put out for garbage.

He hit the chair and flew into the air, then crashed to the ground. At the same moment, one of my partners had pulled up in his vehicle, got out and grabbed the suspect. We placed him in the vehicle and drove back to pick up the cover man who'd been running with me.

Next, we headed to the bus terminal to arrest the other suspect who'd sold me marihuana. When we arrived, a couple of Niagara Regional Police cruisers were arriving at the same time. Perfect timing. Without checking with me, they walked up to my cover man and took him into custody. As they were about to place him in handcuffs, I stated that he was the wrong one and pointed toward the second drug suspect.

They told me, "No, we have the right guy." They had received a call that a girl was seen running down the street yelling with a man was chasing after her. I started to laugh.

I explained to them that girl was me. I was chasing after a drug suspect, and the man chasing me was in fact my partner who had asthma. He'd fallen way behind me and a witness thought he was chasing me. The witness gave a perfect description of my partner. What a night!

WHAT we didn't know at the time was why the suspect had started running when he saw me in the van. As it turned out, to make that night even funnier, apparently the suspect had taken a bar of soap, cut it up in pieces, wrapped the pieces in plastic and told people that it was crack. He was ripping people off.

He ran because he thought I knew that I'd been ripped off. And for that, he received two years in jail. At his trial, the judge said that, had it been real crack cocaine, he would have received four years in jail.

*

SHORTLY after that, crack cocaine began showing up everywhere. I assisted on executing a warrant by the OPP intelligence section in Niagara, who had information that a man from the Niagara area was going to transport a kilo of cocaine. Because we could not determine where the drugs would be transported to, we needed to execute a search warrant on that house right away.

Within minutes that the warrant was executed on the house, a gentleman and his wife arrived at the house. He told me his name and that he was the federal drug Crown attorney in Hamilton. He provided a Hamilton address as his residence and stated that his daughter lived at this house. Imagine that the drug Crown from Hamilton was visiting the same house where a kilo of cocaine had just been seized. I'd be having another encounter with that Crown soon enough.

Chapter Twenty-Two

🍁

THE MOST INTERESTING PART ABOUT conducting a search warrant is the actual search. It's like a game of hide and seek. Who's better at it—the drug dealer (hider) or the police (seeker)? There were many times we won, but also many times we lost. Drug dealers are excellent at finding hiding places and ways to hide their dope.

When I first started working in the Drug Section, I thought the guys were just being mean when they would open the cupboard, take out a box of cereal and empty it into the sink. Time and time again, however drugs were hidden inside cereal boxes. Usually marihuana or cigarettes were hidden in freezers to keep them from going bad.

During one search, we found an unopened can of pop in the fridge. For some reason, the guys thought it seemed wrong so one of them lifted it and shock it and indeed it just didn't feel right. It appeared that the drug dealer had cut the lid off the can with a razor blade, filled in the can with concrete, then placed a pill bottle inside the can and glued the top of the pill bottle to the top of the can. A perfect hiding place, or so he thought.

I used that can during drug talks to show people just how smart drug dealers were at hiding drugs. I've also seen cocaine hidden inside of dread-locks. I thought that was a new way to hide it until one of the Drug Section guys told me that he'd seen that trick to hide drugs in the 1970s. Everything old is new again.

ON one job we did a "controlled delivery" of a machine part that had arrived from Columbia. A controlled delivery is where we take the drugs out of the item, leaving only a sample of the drugs in the package.

The machine part was X-rayed, revealing about a kilo of cocaine located inside. The part was taken to our forensic lab and the drugs were removed. We left one gram of cocaine inside the part, put Malachite green on the inside of the machine part and put it back together again.

Malachite green is a powdery substance that turns green once you mix it with water. If the person receiving the machine part had nothing to do with the drugs hidden inside, there would be no reason for him to take it apart. But if he knew the drugs were hidden inside, he'd get the Malachite green all over his hands.

Then I, dressed as a delivery person, deliver the package. We waited a few minutes, then we executed a search warrant and there he was, the male who had signed for the package, standing in front of us with the greenest hands I had ever seen. We joking called him Kermit the Frog. When he was placed under arrest, he denied any knowledge of the drugs. Of course he did! He was later found guilty of possession of cocaine for the purpose of trafficking.

ANOTHER time we received a call from customs at the Hamilton Airport. They'd recovered a wooden crate containing dishes. The wood used in the crate had been hollowed out and filled with cocaine. I went and picked up the crate and brought it back to see if we could get the drugs out of the wood to allow us to try a controlled delivery to the name of the subject on the receipt.

The forensic guy looked at the crate and was impressed with what a good job the person had done putting the cocaine inside the wood pieces. The wood was cut in two, hollowed out, then filled with cocaine and glued back together. It was almost impossible to tell that the wood had been cut. If it hadn't been for the X-ray, this guy would never have been caught.

Around that same time, we were called to Toronto as a guy from Hamilton had been caught smuggling drugs inside a surfboard. Once again, the drugs were so well hidden that only the X-ray picked up images of the drugs inside.

DRUGS were a dangerous business, not only for the police and criminals themselves, but also sometimes for innocent bystanders. In Niagara Falls, a sudden death case became a drug smuggling investigation when a cab driver was found dead in his home. An autopsy showed the cause of death as a cocaine overdose. A day or so later another cab driver was taken to emergency. He too had a cocaine overdose. Luckily, the second cab driver survived.

Apparently, the first cab driver had picked up a fare in Buffalo, New York, and driven them back into Canada. After he dropped off his passenger, the cab driver found a package containing two bottles of alcohol, one of rum and the other whiskey. Since the cab driver didn't drink whiskey, he gave the bottle to his friend, the second cab driver. Imagine their luck, each getting a free bottle of booze.

That night after finishing his shift the first cab driver decided to have a drink of rum from his new-found bottle. Evidently, he liked to drink his booze straight. No water, ice or mix. He died almost instantly. His friend liked to mix his alcohol with pop. And that's what doctors claimed saved his life.

The police interviewed the surviving driver, who swore he never used drugs. When asked what he ate or drank, he told them about the bottle of alcohol his friend had given him. The police went to the second cab driver's house and found the bottle of whiskey, then took it back to the office and had it tested. It turned out to be liquid cocaine mixed with alcohol. The other bottle was tested and it was exactly the same. Thankfully, no one else was injured or died as a result. It could have been a lot worse.

ONE of the most interesting concealments I ever saw was cocaine hidden inside a laptop computer. The fascinating part was that the laptop still worked. Yet again, we gave thanks to X-ray machine for finding the drugs. The scariest part of that seizure was that instead of drugs, an explosive substance could have been easily been placed inside the laptop.

Years ago, before going through screening at the airport, you'd be asked to turn your computer on. Just turning them on doesn't prove they don't contain drugs. Unfortunately, as the smugglers come up with newer ways of concealing drugs, it takes us much longer to improve the equipment to catch them.

BODY concealment of drugs is definitely the least fun to catch. Drug swallowing is as popular a technique to conceal drugs today as ever before. In the good old days, we'd give the swallowers something to encourage them to go the washroom. As it turns out, if you wait long enough, as they say, "Shit happens!" Condoms full of cocaine, heroin, pills—you name it, it would come out. They would "deposit" their waste in waterless tanks and we would have to retrieve it. It was truly a shitty job!

Eventually, we got the Super Loo—a fancy toilet the swallower would deposit the drugs in, where they would get rinsed and then dropped into a holding tank. Much nicer! The problem occurred when the drugs would leak out or the condom would break. This usually meant death for the carrier. Unless the person is in the hospital at the time it breaks, there is almost no chance for survival.

The other problem is that swallowers will often refuse medical treatment, such as surgery to remove the drugs, or taking a laxative to help move the drugs out of the body. Once a person refuses medical treatment, all we can do it wait. A doctor's hands are tied and so are ours. It's not as if drugs are worth dying for, but for some reason people don't think that way. It's not like we are going to let them go without surrendering the drugs to us. They're not going anywhere until they make that "delivery" and then they're not going anywhere good after that.

DURING one case in Niagara, a man smuggling cocaine into Canada had a medical issue and believed the condom had leaked and he was having an overdose. He went to the hospital and told the doctor that he'd swallowed condoms full of cocaine. It turned out he was actually having a panic attack.

The doctor advised the man it was in his best interests to have the drugs surgically removed. He refused medical treatment, but in the meantime the hospital had called the police and he was arrested for importing drugs and was handcuffed to the hospital bed with an officer assigned to guard him. When he finally passed the condoms, he stuffed them down the socks he was wearing. Somehow, he thought the smell wouldn't be noticed.

ONE particularly awful case was that of a woman who'd gone to a third world country and had the cocaine medically inserted into her breasts. The person had cut open her breasts from underneath and taken out tissue to make room for the drugs.

During the flight her breasts had started to bleed. When she landed she appeared to be bleeding to death. Can you imagine how desperate she must have been to allow a person to cut her open in order to smuggle back cocaine? She could have died and for what? A few thousand dollars.

*

SHAMEFULLY, I have heard of drugs hidden in babies' diapers, and even inside cats, dogs and horses. I have a soft spot for babies and animals, who can't say no. They are the worst kind of victims- as if their lives don't matter. They are just the container used to bring in drugs.

One of the most inventive ones I ever saw was where the drugs were soaked into the clothing. When the clothing was washed, the drugs would come out. Body packers usually place the drugs against their bodies and try to conceal it with their clothes. We all know about people who come back after holidays with a few extra pounds from eating at the buffet. Well, this is a bit different. The body packer straps drugs to legs, arms, around the waist, in their underwear, shoes, hats, and luggage. Believing the extra weight can easily be passed off as a few extra holiday pounds.

You name it, we have seen it. I always said that if drug dealers put their energy toward good deeds instead of bad, they could really improve the world. Instead, I'm sure the game of hide and seek will continue for years to come.

Chapter Twenty-Three

🍁

MY FIRST EXPERIENCE WITH A K9[12] was during a raid at a bar in Niagara Falls. The SWAT team had entered the bar followed by the dog hander and K9. The next thing I saw was a member of the Niagara Police Service come out holding onto his arm. The K9 had attacked and bitten him!

I don't remember which agency owned the dog, but knew it wasn't the RCMP or Canada Customs. The RCMP didn't have any K9 in the province of Ontario—it would take another fifteen to twenty years before we obtained one. Niagara Police service didn't have any either. So when we required the use of a K9 in drug raids, we usually asked Canada Customs, who were the closest service that had a drug detection K9.

Because Canada Customs would use the drug detection dogs at the four border crossings located in the Niagara Region, a K9 was not always available to us. On one night, though, while we were getting ready for a drug raid and contacted Canada Customs, we were advised that the K9 was available and would attend the house being searched in about forty minutes. In the meantime, we started our own search.

Sitting by the front door was a Coleman cooler, and inside that cooler was approximately thirty pounds of marihuana. Searching the inside of

---

12   Police dog

the house, we found more marihuana in the living room, hidden inside a secret compartment located in the fireplace, and ended up completing our search before the K9 had arrived.

When the K9 Unit finally arrived, we advised the handler that we'd already located the drugs, but he asked if he could still work his dog and search for the drugs anyway, requested us not to disclose the location or the type. We agreed, just in case we'd missed anything.

As they got ready to do their search, the K9 lifted his leg and peed on the Coleman Cooler that contained the marihuana, but the dog didn't indicate there were drugs inside. Next, they entered the house and completed their search. Again, the dog didn't indicate there were any drugs inside the house. Confused, the handler asked if we'd removed the drugs, which we hadn't, and wanted to know the type of drugs found. Opening the Coleman Cooler, we showed him the thirty pounds of marihuana. He couldn't believe it, and asking about the drugs located inside the house, we confirmed they were also marihuana.

At this point, the handler had us tell him which room the drugs were in since he wanted to go back in to search again. Having revealed their location, the handler took his dog back into the living room and searched it again, but once more, the dog didn't indicate any drugs. Lastly, he asked whereabouts in the living room the drugs were hidden, and had his dog re-search the fireplace area. But again, the dog didn't indicate. Even when we showed the handler the exact spot where the drugs were and he took his dog to the location, the dog would not indicate.

It was obvious that the handler was embarrassed. And it was apparent we couldn't be relying completely on a K9 to locate drugs.

SINCE the Customs K9 wasn't indicating on the drugs, we started searching for other options, and located a dog trainer who claimed his dog could locate drugs, guns and explosives. So we asked to meet with him and see his dog in action. We drove out to his training location and he showed us a Belgian Malinois, which looked like a German Shepherd. The trainer placed his dog in a secure vehicle while they hid several packages containing drugs, and then we watched as he worked his dog, who located every package that he'd hidden. Pleased with what we'd observed, we asked the trainer to come to our office and do the same presentation for the Drug Section Commander.

On the day of the presentation, the trainer, who was also the dog handler, came up to our office, bringing copies of his résumé and training certificates. The handler asked the Drug Section Commander to hide three packages of drugs anywhere in the office, then call him in once they were hidden. The commander went to the drug vault and pulled out three packages: one containing cocaine, one containing marihuana and another containing LSD. We watched him hide the drugs around the office. A few minutes later, we called the handler to come in with the dog and search the office.

One by one, the dog found the packages that the commander had hidden, but to all of our surprise, the dog indicated more than just the three places. In fact, the dog had indicated at a desk that we didn't hide any drugs in. Of course, we were very disappointed by the fourth indication as we believed the dog was wrong.

Noting this, the handler asked what was wrong and we admitted we'd only hid three packages. Sure his dog was right, he asked us to search the desk, and as we opened the desk drawer, there sitting inside was a package containing cocaine. It turned out that a member had worked late and hadn't placed the drugs inside a temporary exhibit locker. The dog was right after all! And we had found our new drug dog.

Because the handler and his dog were not law enforcement officers, this meant that every time we intended to use them during a drug raid, we'd have to ask for permission to use them in the warrant. And use them we did. The tougher the search, the funnier it was to watch them work.

*

WE had received information from Crime Stoppers that there was some drug trafficking at the Fort Erie Race Track, so we conducted drug searches on the premises. As this is a race track for horses, the conditions were less then idea. While we were searching one of the rider's quarters, though, the dog started indicating and scratching at the wooden floorboards. The hander searched the wood board and found *one* marihuana seed. WOW!

Another time, acting on a Crime Stoppers tip, we took the dog handler and dog to a big field located behind Brock University in St. Catharines. The tip alleged there were several large marihuana plants growing here. The field was huge and was full of overgrown bushes. Once again, the conditions were not idea, but the handler agreed to find, so he released the dog and we followed. We walked and walked, and just as we were ready to call off the search, the dog indicated. We located about fifty of the nicest marihuana plants I'd ever seen!

We used them again on another Crime stoppers tip where marihuana was supposedly growing in a field behind a school. Having located about ten to fifteen marihuana plants, we cut them down and I left my business card on the stick used to support one of the plants. On the card I wrote, *If you want to claim these, please call.* Obviously, I never heard from any one.

A year later, we'd received a tip that marihuana was being grown in the backyard of a house. So we obtained a search warrant and located several small marihuana plants. Inside the house, sitting on top of the fireplace mantel was my business card with my written message on it. *Well, well, hello there!* I ended up seizing my own business card as evidence against the suspect.

Chapter Twenty-Four

♦

IN THE FALL OF 1992, I was sent to an Expert Witness Conference hosted by the Toronto Police Service. It consisted of a panel which included Alan Greenspan, a judge and a prosecutor. Several officers from around the province attended.

During this conference, I met a member from the Ottawa Drug section whom I'd never met before. He was extremely nice and friendly. After a couple of days at the conference, this member phoned my room and asked if he could come up to my room to discuss a part of the conference.

He came to my room and sat in a chair in the corner of the room by the window. Asking if I had anything to drink, I said that I didn't but we could go to the bar. As I got up to walk toward the door, he grabbed me forcefully from behind and pushed me onto the bed face down. He pulled down my track pants and underwear while holding me painfully by the hair and forcing my face into the bed. He then violently anally raped me. I felt such a searing pain that I couldn't even scream. I was barely able to breathe.

All I could do was feel the excruciating pain.

When he was finished, I rolled into the fetal position and lay as still as I could on the bed in total shock. He got up and walked out of my room.

I stayed there for what felt like an hour. I was in so much pain I could hardly stand up. I went to the bathroom and took a shower to wash myself, as I felt dirty. I felt like it was my fault for letting this member in my room.

For the next few days, I couldn't walk without severe pain and couldn't sit at all. I wore menstrual pads to stem the bleeding.

DURING one of the breaks the next day, a female RCMP officer from the Ottawa Drug Section happened to warn me about this member and said that he wasn't a very nice person. I only wished that she had warned me the day before and maybe this wouldn't have happened, since I wouldn't have allowed him to meet me in my room.

For the rest of the conference I walked around in a daze, trying not to reveal that I was in pain because I didn't want anyone to ask me about it, and working hard to avoid the member who'd assaulted me. To this day, I don't remember that member's name, except that it was French. The scariest part is that I can't even remember what he looked like. My whole career was based on being able to describe the person I'd bought drugs from, but I was too stunned to be able to do the same about the person who brutally assaulted me. For years I never told anyone about this assault as I was ashamed and felt like it was my own fault for letting him into my room.

I was a different person after this assault. I'd endured many small acts of abuse by members before this, and had always managed to overcome their sting, but this left me a changed woman. I started to stay away from friends and coworkers. I fell into a depression. I cried a lot at home and at times thought about killing myself. I told my doctor that I was depressed and he prescribed medication for depression. The medication made me feel worse so I stopped taking it. I knew something was wrong with me, but I felt I had no choice except to keep moving forward. It I let this eat me up, my career would be over. So I buried it and tried to forget about it.

Over time, I thought I had wiped it from my mind. I'd moved on, or so I thought. Several years later, it would come back to almost ruin my life. It was twenty years before I would tell anyone about that terrible day.

IN late 1992, yet another issue was about to change my life. A new Commanding Officer in charge of the RCMP in Ontario decided that it was time to move members around. Letters were sent to the members telling them that they were going to be transferred and told them where they could possibly be transferred to. I received my letter and it advised that I was to be transferred to Sault Ste. Marie or Sudbury. Of course, I wasn't anxious to transfer. I was still trying to recover from the rape and wanted to stay in Niagara where I could at least stay close to my best friend.

It appeared that more than half of all the members had received a letter. I'd never seen anything like this in my years of service. I knew that in contract provinces members usually move every three to four years, but we had members who'd been stationed in Niagara for eighteen to twenty years, yet they didn't receive these transfer letters.

I advised Staffing that after years of working undercover, I wanted to stay in Niagara and start working as an investigator on drug files and did not want a transfer at this time. Then I received a second letter stating that I would be transferred to Toronto Airport. I'd worked at the airport during the Gulf War when it was mainly security detail and not a lot of investigative work or related to my drug training and experience. So I repeated my request to remain in Niagara as it seemed to be in line with the way other officers from that detachment were being treated.

Within a week or so, I received a phone call from Staffing, advising me that there was an opening for a female undercover drug position in Hamilton and asked if I would take that transfer. I asked what my options were. Staffing told me that if I didn't take the transfer to Hamilton Drug

Section, I was going to be transferred to the airport. I asked if I could have the weekend to think about it.

When I got off the phone, I went to talk to the sergeant and told him what Staffing had said. He said that Hamilton Drug Section was much better than the airport and recommended that I not fight the transfer and just go to Hamilton. I decided to take his advice, but I was devastated. I thought he would ask me to stay and fight the transfer. He was like a father to me. Telling me to go, broke my heart. On that Monday, I phoned Staffing and agreed to take the move to Hamilton.

IT ended up that many members fought their transfer notices and filed grievances. As a result, most if not all transfers were cancelled. Again, I was devastated because I'd been told I had no choice but to go.

If I'd stayed and fought, I could have remained in Niagara. I was angry with the sergeant about that for a long time. I'd given him so much, worked so hard and had taken so many risks to make the Drug Section look good, and yet felt my concerns were not taken into consideration. It felt like a rejection. A transfer party was held and I cried.

Chapter Twenty-Five

🍁

IN MAY 1993, I WAS transferred to Hamilton Detachment Drug Section. I commuted back and forth from my house in Niagara to the detachment in downtown Hamilton, and had to drive right past the Niagara Detachment to get to Hamilton. Every day as I drove past it, I would curse the RCMP for forcing me to move.

WHEN I arrived in Hamilton, my supervisor told me not to rock the boat, to slowly ease my way into the section. I'd worked with this member in Niagara and he knew I was a hard worker. Of course, I took this personally and the very next day I made my first arrest.

I was asked to work with a junior member and to teach him some of my drug skills. In time, I taught him how to buy drugs and we would take turns approaching suspected drug dealers and try to buy drugs from them. At one point, the junior member was transferred to the Brantford Joint Forces street team to use his skills in the Brantford area.

ONE of the things I think you should know about the Hamilton Detachment were the working conditions. The detachment was infested with mice. We'd be sitting at our desks and then someone would let out a scream, so we'd all lift our feet off the floor as a mouse ran under our desks.

We complained, but nothing ever seemed to be done about it. Eventually, traps were placed around the detachment and every day they were all full of dead mice.

Once I thought the rodent issue had been fixed, I opened a canteen since there was no place to get food or refreshments after 4:00 pm. It became clear that the issue had not been corrected as the mice (or rats) were eating the food from the canteen. Mars Bars and Vachon Flakies were their favorites. I'd go in every day and clean out the stuff that had been ripped open and partially eaten. Ultimately, we had to close the canteen because the food was being eaten, but the mice weren't paying!

The RCMP office had several other issues as well. The parking garage was dripping with water and the garbage bins were located in the parking area. There was always a foul smell and the water constantly dripped on my car, eating away at the paint. The parking area was also very dark and felt unsafe as the public could easily gain entry. Evidently, years earlier a woman had been killed in the underground parking, which was not a comfort to female members.

SOON after arriving, I was asked to do an undercover job for the Hamilton Wentworth Regional Police. While they would be running the project, an RCMP officer would be my cover man. For about six weeks I worked the job. The primary target, a uniformed police officer.

It was alleged that he was taking money from the Hell's Angels in return for allowing them to sell drugs. As I had just started working in Hamilton, no one from the other police service knew who I was. This job was straight night shifts from 4:00 pm to 12:00 am or even later as required. I wasn't allowed to show up at the RCMP detachment, instead meeting my cover team at various locations in Hamilton.

We targeted bars in the downtown core of Hamilton. It turned out to be just another street drug operation, and the target was nowhere in sight. This was because he'd been on holidays for the first month of the project and nobody thought to tell me. That left little time to investigate him. I only ever saw him once in the bar and he stayed for about five minutes.

The Hamilton team had me attend an area well known for prostitution at one point, wanting to target the taxi drivers. They wanted the cabs to see me disguised as a prostitute working on the corner, but they didn't want to arrest any Johns, just taxi drivers. They told me if I were asked to conduct a sexual act for money to give a really high price as a way of avoiding ever having to do anything sexual. Obviously, I'd never done this before and had no idea what the prices were!

One truck kept driving around and around. Finally, he pulled over and asked, "How much for a blowjob?"

When I said, "$150," he replied that that was very expensive.

I assured him, "I'm worth every penny. Just keep driving around and think about it!"

He drove away and thankfully didn't come back to take me up on it.

AS part of this job I began to hang around a girl I'd met at the bar. I bought her a beer and she told me about her boyfriend who'd slipped and fallen to his death from the same building where the RCMP office is located. It seemed that he'd jumped to his death the day before I started working in that building.

I would buy her drinks and she would sit and talk to me. That allowed some of the drug dealers to see me hanging around with her and gave me credibility. Later, when I approached a guy to buy drugs, he consulted the female I had befriended and asked her if I was okay. She gave me the thumbs up and the man sold me drugs.

*

AT the end of the project, all the suspects that I'd purchased drugs from were arrested. The girl that I hung around with came to the Hamilton Police Station to turn herself in. The police advised her that there was no warrant for her arrest and she was free to go.

She insisted, saying "You have to arrest me. Everyone thinks I'm a rat." Because she'd stood up for me and told people they could trust me, they had sold me drugs, and now they were blaming her. Although I'd never purchased drugs from her—and I don't think she sold drugs—she felt that my actions had put her in danger. Unfortunately, there was nothing the police could do for her. I felt so badly about that. I'd never intended for that to happen.

In the end, there wasn't enough information to lay any charges against the target officer, but the Hamilton Wentworth Police confronted the officer about the allegations and told him that an undercover project had been conducted to prove or disprove the allegations. For reasons unknown to me, they actually told him that I was the undercover officer. In undercover work, the name of the undercover officer is not released to the suspects until court. Because there were no charges, my true identity should never have been released. The officer was never truly cleared of the allegations and he could be corrupt. Giving my identity to the officer put me at risk, and he did soon confront me at the detachment, demanding to know why I'd targeted him. Not only did I have to keep clear of the people I had arrested, but now also for this officer. I couldn't understand why the Hamilton Wentworth Police would expose me to such an unnecessary threat.

Chapter Twenty-Six

🍁

WHEN I RETURNED TO MY regular duties at Hamilton Drug Section, my first supervisor had been transferred out and I was assigned a new supervisor. From the start, he was very friendly and professional. He lived in Grimsby, and because I was commuting from Niagara Falls every day, he offered to help pay for my parking if I would pick him up and drop him off from work. This made good sense, so I agreed. After a couple of months, he started making comments about his sex life, marriage, and family.

As the supervisor, he made up the shifts and decided who worked together—I was always assigned to work with him. Members noticed that we were always paired together and started to leave things on my desk. One day, there was a roll of toilet paper left with a note on it implying that I was—sucking up to the supervisor.

At first, I tried to laugh it off, but then got very angry, and threatened to have it fingerprinted and have the member charged with harassment. I didn't choose to work with my supervisor, I was ordered to work with him.

ONCE again, I was asked to buy drugs on the streets of Hamilton. I was working undercover one night and purchased some marihuana from a man. Then after a couple of weeks, we went back and arrested him. Asking him if he knew who I was, he said he remembered selling me some weed. I revealed I was a police officer and that he was under arrest.

We took him back to our office where he was searched. I was handed his wallet, and when I looked inside, there was a pay stub from the Hamilton Tigercats football team. I asked him if he was a football player and he confirmed that he was. When I asked why he was selling pot, he used the old story that they weren't his drugs, but his friend's and was doing him a favour.

Since it was obvious that he wanted to have a professional football career, I informed him that by selling drugs he wouldn't be allowed to enter the United States.

When I arrived to testify at his trial, I met the Crown. This was the same Crown attorney who'd attended a drug house in Niagara a couple of years before. The Crown told me that I was not required to testify and when I asked the reason, he told me the accused had pled guilty to one count of possession. I was dismayed and reminded him that the charge was trafficking, not possession. The Crown had offered him the deal. I sarcastically asked him if he'd gotten seasons tickets out of the deal.

Later that season, the accused was running the ball down the field and was ready to score the winning touchdown, when he dropped the ball and the other team recovered it. Hamilton was out of the playoffs! I smiled. Karma.

ON March 15, 1994, my supervisor and I flew to New York to interview a source on a drug file. After the meetings were held, we had dinner and went to our separate rooms. I was watching TV when there was a knock at my door. I answered, and there was my supervisor standing in the hallway wearing just his underwear.

He walked into my room and tried to kiss me. I told him I wasn't interested in a sexual relationship with him. He said he'd forgotten his room key and asked to sleep on the bed until the morning. But again, he tried to kiss me and said he wanted to sleep with me. I repeated I was not interested and it wasn't until I told him that I was on my menstrual period did he stop pushing himself on me.

He slept on the bed beside me. I was afraid that he would still try to attack me. I was scared and didn't know what to do. I didn't sleep, as I feared he would attack me. There seemed to be no end to these types of situations for a female in the RCMP.

ON another occasion after this incident, my supervisor opened his work briefcase, revealing that he had a package of condoms. After this incident, I knew I had to get away from my supervisor before things escalated into another assault.

I put my house up for sale, but the real estate market in Niagara had dropped. I decided that even though I was going to lose money, I couldn't continue to commute with my supervisor after what had happened in New York. He obviously could not take "No!" for an answer.

I ended up moving to Brantford on a temporary bases until I could find a new place to live. I didn't travel in the same direction as he did anymore and, therefore, didn't have to commute with him again.

Chapter Twenty-Seven

❦

BY THIS TIME, I'D BEEN declared an expert witness in the area of drugs. As an expert witness, the Crown prosecutor sends you the exhibit report and a brief summary of the case. I then decide whether or not I believe, based on my experience, the suspect was a dealer, and what level the dealer was, whether a street level, mid- level or high level.

When you are called to give expert witness testimony, a judge must declare you an expert each and every time you appear in court. This requires that you attend court with your résumé outlining your experience, and testify before the judge by answering questions about your expertise from the Crown and defence attorneys and sometimes by the judge. You need to prove every time to each new judge that you have knowledge about drugs, prices, packaging, street terms for drugs, and that you have training, as well as experience purchasing drugs. The defence then has a chance to cross-examine you. Once both sides have questioned you, the judge will decide if you are an expert or not. I was always declared an expert witness.

Expert witness testimony is very different from testifying on a case. During a case you give the evidence based on your memories and the notes you take to help refresh your memory. As an expert, you already know what you're going to say because you've already reviewed the evidence and prepared your testimony.

The funniest question I was ever asked by a judge was, "Officer, how many marihuana buds does a marihuana plant produce?" Well, that is like asking how many roses a rose bush will produce? It depends! It depends on the health of the plant, soil, watering, amount of sunlight, fertilizers, etc.

*

ONE day, I was walking with a friend to my car to drive home to Brantford. While walking toward the parking area, I saw a person that I'd purchased drugs from. I could tell that he recognized me too. I told my friend to keep walking toward the car and wait for me there, but to act like she didn't know me. Then I walked away from my friend and back toward the detachment.

This suspect had been very upset when he found out I was a cop and I was worried that there might be trouble. I returned to the detachment and he waited outside for a few minutes and then left. That's always a concern when you do an undercover job in the same city that you work—that someone will spot you, follow you or worse, hurt you.

Following that incident, I decided to get my long hair cut very short, in hopes that people wouldn't recognize me. It was another reminder that I had many enemies. I needed to be careful.

IN June, I was seconded to work on a Joint Forces Operation with HWPD [13]and the OPP. This was good news because it allowed me to keep away from the problematic supervisor. This project was a wiretap investigation against a traditional, organized crime group in Hamilton that involved the importation of hundreds of kilos of cocaine from the United States into Canada. At last, I could enhance my investigation skills. I loved investigating!

In the case of a wiretap investigation, a warrant is brought before a

---

13   Hamilton Wentworth Police Department later became the Hamilton Police Service

judge to ask for the authority to listen and record conversations. After the judge reads the warrant, he will either sign it to give us the authority or will deny it. Once the authority is granted, it is only allowed for ninety days, after which another warrant must be prepared to continue listening and recording.

*

ONE day, while listening to a conversation at a target's place of work, it came over the lines that an RCMP member had visited the business and had flashed his badge to try to get a discount. I brought this matter to the officer in charge of Hamilton Detachment, and that member was called in and spoken to.

I was embarrassed because the Hamilton Police and OPP were there to overhear that conversation too. Later, I would have a run-in with that member. He was upset that I reported this incident.

Also during the investigation, we overheard a conversation from the main target that he had informants in the Hamilton Wentworth Police Department, and if it weren't for them, he would be in jail by now. Now it was their turn to be embarrassed. The Hamilton Police were able to determine where one of the leaks was located, but couldn't act on it since it would put their source at risk.

This project lasted well over a year, followed by several months of disclosure and bail hearings. The primary target was arrested along with fourteen other suspects. The other good news was that, by the time this project was finished, my supervisor had been moved to another area.

DURING this project, a friend and her daughter moved into my home due to personal issues. It turned out that my friend's first husband, who had married a lady from Hamilton, was a close associate of the prime suspect in my investigation. I found this out at my home when he came over to make sure his daughter was settled into her new residence. That was a very stressful time as now the prime suspect could find out where I lived.

Having my friend and her daughter live with me, though, ended up being a good thing. Now I had people to look out for and that meant I wouldn't take as many risks as I had in the past. Having people in my life changed how I behaved in dangerous situations. There had been a time when I didn't care if I lived or died.

Dying on duty was always a possibility, but now if I died, they would be homeless. They gave me something to live for and became my adopted family. I am so grateful that they have stayed in my life. After so many years of having no connections, this was a very positive change.

IN 1995, I did an undercover job for Kitchener Detachment as they needed a female undercover officer. I was briefed by a member that an informant knew someone who'd just been arrested and who had a kilo of cocaine to sell. The informant had told the suspect that he knew a female stripper who might buy the cocaine, and had described the stripper as being well-endowed and having long blonde hair.

I told the member that I'd cut my hair short, but decided the informant could say I'd worn a wig when I was stripping. As for the well-endowed part, I would have to be more creative. A friend of mine suggested that we should try to stuff a bra, then wear a loose top and leggings to see if we could create the right look, so we did. My next-door neighbour was a great guy so I phoned him and asked if I could come over. He took one look at me and his reaction was perfect! I knew I had found the look.

On the date that I was to be in Kitchener to make the deal, I dressed up in my "costume" and drove to the detachment. I'd never been there before and I didn't know any of the detachment members. I arrived, went to the detachment lobby, and asked for the name of the officer I was to meet.

Coincidentally during this time, an officer I had worked with in Niagara came out of the front door. He recognized me and said, "Oh Paulette, can I touch them?" He knew me well enough to know they were fake.

Sadly, my efforts had been wasted because the suspect was in jail and he no longer had access to the cocaine. No deal.

ON another occasion, I was asked by Hamilton Wentworth Police to assist them with the arrest of a suspect. They asked me to go into an apartment and get the suspect to come out so they could arrest him. I was on my way to the office and didn't have my pistol with me, but agreed to do it anyway. I said I'd try to make an undercover buy from him to get him to come out.

I entered the building and climbed up thirty or forty stairs to the landing. It was dark and narrow. When I knocked on the door and asked for the suspect, the man who'd answered the door said that was him. I asked to purchase a gram of cocaine, reached into my pocket and took out some money. He told me to wait while he went into the apartment and came back out. He asked to see the money and I asked to see the cocaine.

That's when I noticed that he had something in his right hand. The next thing I knew, the suspect swung out at me with what appeared to be a knife. The knife grazed my face, and I grabbed his arm. The fight was on.

By this point, the officers from HWPD arrived, hit the suspect with a baton and arrested him. The whole time I'd been hanging on to his arm to prevent him from stabbing me again. I'd received a small cut on my left cheek, but I was very lucky not to have received a more serious injury. When the media covered the story and reported that a female undercover officer had been stabbed, I had to contact a lot of people to tell them I was allright and that I hadn't actually been stabbed.

*

AT that time, I was also working on a project that involved an organized crime group engaged in the cultivation of marihuana. One of the informants advised us that a Hamilton Wentworth police officer was implicated in this illegal activity. When I turned this information over to the Hamilton Wentworth Internal Affairs, they already had an investigation ongoing into this matter. And they also provided me with information that they were investigating one of the RCMP officers at Hamilton Detachment, but didn't disclose the name of the person they were investigating. This meant there was someone I worked with who could not be trusted.

In addition to this, I also provided Internal Affairs with information on another officer who I believed had perjured himself on a drug case. Hamilton Wentworth commenced an investigation into this member, and as a result, I had to provide a statement to the Niagara Regional Police who'd been called to investigate this matter. Shortly afterward, the members of Hamilton Wentworth police told me that I'd crossed the "Blue Line" and sarcastically wished me good luck if l ever needed backup.

I didn't take this seriously at first because they were mad at me for coming forward. It wasn't until later that an employee from Immigration Canada told me that she'd been warned to stay away from me if she wanted Hamilton Wentworth Police assistance on any future cases. She took their warning seriously and didn't call me to assist her on any further cases. At least she was brave enough to tell me the truth.

On another occasion, I had to bring some disclosure over to a member of the Hamilton Wentworth police and was told that I was no longer welcome to attend their office. At that point, I'd become very concerned about my safety, so I approached a member from a different section and asked if he would switch places with me. This would take me out of the Drug Section and away from the risk of working with HWPS.

I also approached the Drug NCO about a transfer, advising him that I no longer felt safe working with the HWPD, and a transfer was granted. I felt betrayed for doing the right thing and as a result I felt forced to leave the Drug Section for my own safety and that of my fellow coworkers who had to continue to work with the HWPD. This was not the first time I would learn that the whistleblower is the one who pays the most.

Chapter Twenty-Eight

🍁

IN MAY OF 1996, I was transferred to the FES[14] of the RCMP. Looking for a fresh start and new duties, I was disappointed when I found out that yet again they wanted me to work undercover, this time purchasing counterfeit goods, CDs, videos, satellite dishes, etc. This was the work I was trying to get away from, but it appeared to follow me wherever I went.

There was, however, one nice thing about working in FES: one part of our duties was to attend the gravesites of deceased RCMP members to ensure they were well-maintained. This struck me as a nice touch, just knowing that members are still remembered after they are gone.

ONE day, I'd been required to testify on a drug case in Welland, and when I was driving back to Hamilton after the case was finished, I was passed by a convertible sports car with the top down, weaving in and out of traffic. I radioed in the licence plate, but because the car was speeding, I'd almost lost sight of it by the time our dispatch reported that the car was stolen.

I tried my best to keep up with the car, but at this point, it was the end of the workday and traffic was very heavy. Of course, the car I was driving didn't have emergency lights or sirens. All I had was a single detachable red light that you could put on the top of the car and I didn't want to use that

---

14   Federal Enforcement Section

light since the RCMP dispatch had connected me with the OPP dispatch—
I was giving continuous updates as to speed and exits as we passed them
by. I was told that the OPP would take over the pursuit just before the
Skyway Bridge near Hamilton.

As we approached the bridge, I could see a number of OPP cruisers
merging onto the highway and I watched as the OPP tried to box in the
stolen car travelling in the fast lane. They maneuvered one cruiser in front
of the stolen convertible, one behind it and one beside it. Then all of a
sudden, the stolen car turned onto the far-left shoulder of the road and I
saw a lot of dust and smoke. Calling over the radio that I thought there'd
been an accident, the next thing I saw was the stolen car cutting across
all the lanes of traffic to the right to take the exit before the bridge. They
had lost the car and the pursuit was called off due to the danger to other
motorists. That was so exciting, yet disappointing that the vehicle got away.

LATER on, I was asked to assist the Customs and Excise team. One of
the jobs we worked on was buying cigarettes from a suspect on the Six
Nations Reserve, and I was teaching another female member how to purchase illegal cigarettes and alcohol. So we attended a garage and asked to
buy alcohol. Once we'd gained entry, I observed a loaded shotgun leaning
against the door. Obviously, these guys meant business.

We purchased a couple of bottles of alcohol and informed them that
we wanted to buy much more in a couple of weeks as we were organizing a
wedding and wanted to get the booze from them. He agreed and gave us a
price, and when we arrived the next time, we purchased twenty-five bottles
of liquor. The suspect had packed the bottles up in dog food boxes in case
we got pulled over so that it would look like we had dog food, not booze.

At the end of this project, though, no charges were laid against the
guys who'd sold us the liquor. This was a slap in our faces. We felt we'd put

ourselves at risk, but no one wanted to lay charges against the natives.

*

WHILE I was in FES, I was asked to act as a Native Liaison Officer along with another member for the Six Nations Reserve. We were tasked to organize a canoe trip with the Six Nations Police, taking twelve students for a three-day canoe trip down the Grand River, starting at the Elora Gorge and ending at Chiefswood Park at the Six Nations Reserve. The goal was to expose the students to some of the native traditions, such as canoeing, and other aspects of the culture.

But before we could attempt such a trip, we had to complete the trip without the students just to see if it were actually viable.

We planned to portage the canoes and all our gear (sleeping bags, clothes, food) over two dams and stay at camping sites near the Grand River. So, off we went.

Due to the river being so low, we started our trip in Kitchener instead of Elora. The first day, we paddled down the river, having to portage once. It ended up being a lot more work than we had anticipated. We stopped in Cambridge for the night at a campsite, where we once again had to portage our canoes and gear across the road into the park. Then we hauled everything back across the road in the morning and paddled our way toward Brantford where, yet again, we had to portage, this time at the Paris Dam. Boy this was hard work.

As we made our way to Brantford, once more we had to portage around another dam, then got back into the water and finally paddled our way toward Six Nations.

By this point, we were so exhausted that we stopped and called in the troops to come and pick us up. There was no way we could finish, and there was no way we could do this with twelve students.

Debriefing our trip, we decided that the only way we could make the trip possible was to have a van carry our tents, food and gear. That way, we would paddle and portage only and the van would meet us at the next stop with the gear. In the mornings, the van would bring in breakfast for the group, then we'd pack up the van and start paddling again. After all was said and done, we did make the trip and the students had an experience of a lifetime, although not necessarily doing it the traditional way.

IN 1996, the Ontario government made a change that women could go topless in public swimming pools. Within a day or two of this ruling, a member approached me in the office, in front of several members and said, "Go ahead, Paulette, show us your tits."

Trying once again to be one of the guys, I responded that I would do so only after he dropped his pants. And only then if I could stop laughing long enough to undo my blouse.

Nonetheless, the comment was uncalled for and I'd not engaged that member prior to his making the comment. This was the same member who'd used his badge to try to get a discount. It wasn't unusual for that member to make these types of comments and it put female officers in a constant state of alert among their own colleagues. When he made sexual comments to another female member in front of other members, she filed a complaint, but it appeared that no action was ever taken against him.

Just around this time, the harassment issue was getting some attention in the RCMP.

The OIC[15] at the detachment put out some communications stating that pictures of the Sunshine Girls were no longer appropriate in the office, yet each day the pictures would still be posted in the office . The OIC would

---

15   Officer in Charge

come along and take the photos down, and the next day a new picture would be put up. This took place over several weeks.

At one point, a member of the Drug Section approached me and said if I put up a firefighter calendar, nothing would be done either. Of course, the females never displayed such calendars or pictures.

SOON I received another request to do an undercover job in Kitchener. They needed females to act as girlfriends to some undercover men who had already met the female target. Since the target was cool toward the men, they were hoping the "girlfriends" could get close to her.

I arrived at the safe house and met the undercover officers. Then two other female undercover officers attended as well. We were to have a house party that night and invite the target so that she could meet us. All went well and we met the target.

During the party, she invited us to come to her apartment for drinks and we went. There, she served us shots of Sambuca and invited us to come back another time to go out to her favourite bar.

The team was excited because that was the same bar where her biker gang friends hung out, so myself and another female officer agreed to do it.

The next time we were to attend the target's apartment, both of us had worked our regular day shift, and then had to drive to Kitchener to work the undercover job. As it turned, out neither of us had eaten dinner. The other operator had purchased a bag of Doritos, and, well, that was supper.

Arriving at the target's apartment, where we met two other women, she served everyone two shots of Sambuca and then we headed out to the bar. Of course, by then on an empty stomach, I was already feeling the shots' effects.

We accompanied the suspect to the bar, and once there, she told the waitress, "Every time I raise my hand, I want you to bring a round of

Sambuca for everyone at the table."

As the waitress was walking away, I got up and said I was going to the bathroom. I followed the waitress, and when the suspect couldn't see us, I approached her and asked, "How would you like to make some extra money tonight? Every time she raises her hand to order shots of Sambuca, bring me water but charge her for the drink. I'm the designated driver, but she wants me to drink, so don't tell her." The waitress agreed.

So throughout the night, the suspect kept raising her hand, and I kept getting water.

At the end of the night, we drove back to Kitchener Detachment to do a debriefing. As we started to debrief the evening, the other female officer was very impaired and slurring her words. At some point she asked, "Paulette why aren't you as drunk as I am?" I told her what I'd done, and when she asked why I hadn't done the same thing for her, I explained that it would have been believable if I'd had to justify why I did it—because I was the designated driver—but it wouldn't have been if there were two of us.

Later, as I was driving her home, the poor woman threw up all over herself. I had a jacket in the back of the car and told her to take her soiled top off and put on my jacket, putting her shirt in a plastic bag then in the trunk of the car so I wouldn't have to smell it all the way to her house. When we arrived at her home around 3:00 am, her husband answered the door and I had to tell him that his wife was passed out in the front of the car. He came out and helped her into the house. I handed him the plastic bag containing her dirty shirt and said, "Here you go!"

Two days later I received a parcel in the mail. It was an apology and a freshly cleaned jacket!

Chapter Twenty-Nine

🍁

MY LAST UNDERCOVER JOB WAS in Barrie, Ontario, in 1996. I was to act as a girlfriend for a male UCO [16]who was to make a purchase of drugs. Told to meet the UCO and cover team at a hotel in Barrie, I drove up after working my regular shift and was briefed on the scenario—it was my job to hold onto the buy money. Before leaving the hotel, the UCO asked me if I was carrying any weapons, which I thought was odd, but I told him that I wasn't. He said me the same was true of himself.

We drove together to the bar and I was introduced to the target, but he didn't seem to be that interested in me. After having a drink together, we made the drug transaction and walked out together to the parking lot. Once there, the cover team arrested all three of us, then once the suspect had been taken away, the male UCO and I returned to the hotel where we had to wait for the cover team to process the accused.

While waiting for them, the male UCO offered me a drink. I had a beer. Then he took off his boots and removed a knife and a handgun. I asked him why he hadn't told me he was carrying weapons, explaining that had something happened, I could have used those weapons, and that he'd put me at risk by not telling me. Also, had the target searched him, we both would have been in a risky situation. This was not a safe way for a team to

---

16   Under Cover Officer

work together.

After the cover team arrived and debriefed us, I asked where my room was. Since it was late and we'd been drinking, I assumed that the cover team had booked me a hotel room. They laughed and informed me that I was already in it. I told them I should not be expected to sleep in the same room as the male UCO and they just laughed again and said there was no extra room for me.

I became very upset and left the room to go down and ask at the hotel desk if they had any rooms. They did, so I booked my own room. Returning to the room where the cover team was, I explained to that I'd gotten my own room and that it was inappropriate to expect me to share a room with the male officer. At this point, the male undercovers response was to ask me if I wanted to stay in his room and sleep with him. I was appalled and outraged that he thought I would do so.

THE next day, when I walked out to my car, I found a note under my windshield from the OPP officer who was working with the Barrie team. He'd written to say how sorry he was for what had happened the night before, and for the way I was treated. He left his name and number on the note. I never contacted him.

I didn't report this incident as it was my word against theirs, and previous experience had shown me there was no point. Also, I didn't want to get the OPP officer in trouble. Deciding then and there that I would never put myself in that situation again, I didn't accept any further undercover work. I truly felt that the only reason I'd been asked to participate in this undercover job was to be offered up for sex by the officers involved.

I would be asked to do more undercover work, but I turned them down. Looking back, I can't believe how poisonous the work environment was in the RCMP. I tried so hard to be accepted into the RCMP family, had put myself at risk and endured a lot of stress doing undercover work, only to be left fighting and defending myself against the people who were sworn to serve and protect. It dawned on me that at some points in my career, I felt safer with the suspects I was investigating than with the officers I teamed with.

I was glad that part of my life was over, but at the time I didn't realize the long-term effects the first nine years of my career would have on me.

Chapter Thirty

❦

IT WAS AROUND THIS TIME I attended my first and only "sudden death". Many people think that police officers encounter a lot of dead bodies, and although that's often the case, it wasn't true during my career. The unusual part was that I wasn't even on duty when it happened.

I walked into my doctor's office as I had an appointment and the receptionist told me the doctor would be leaving shortly, but that he wouldn't be gone long, explaining that he'd just been called to a sudden death. Asking her how long he'd be, she estimated about twenty minutes. I decided I had time to wait, so I sat down and waited. As soon as I sat down, my doctor walked out of his office and toward the door. Seeing me sitting there and, knowing what I did for a living, he asked, "Do you want to come with me?"

We drove together in his car and during the drive to the scene, he told me the details. Apparently, the victim's sister had been trying to get in touch with her brother and he hadn't been answering the phone. Knowing that her brother had been depressed and was suicidal, she drove from Toronto, broke into his house and found her brother dead.

When we arrived at the victim's house, I observed the local police guarding the house. The officer stated that the body was downstairs—everyone knew that my doctor was the local coroner—so I followed my doctor and walked to the stairwell. There, I saw an older man lying on the floor at the bottom of the stairs. His one leg was up on the stairs, his body on the floor and there was a small amount of blood on his face between his nose and mouth. On the floor beside him was a book and his glasses neatly folded. He was dressed in pyjamas and a housecoat.

There was no blood spatter, no visible signs of trauma, no signs of a break and enter, except for the window his sister had broken to get inside. My doctor turned to me and asked, "What do you think happened?"

I told him it looked like the victim had gone down the stairs to get a book and had fallen back down the stairs hitting his head on the floor, thus explaining the blood on his face. My doctor agreed that's what it appeared to be but for the fact that there was no wound on the back of his head. After the autopsy, it revealed the victim had had a massive heart attack, and not committed suicide or fallen accidentally.

Chapter Thirty-One

🍁

FOLLOWING THREE MONTHS OF WORKING in the FES, I was approached to see if I'd be interested in a transfer to the CCS[17] since they needed someone with search warrant experience. At first, I was a bit intimidated by the Fraud Section. When the member asked me, "Do you know what the difference is between a $1,000 and a $100,000 fraud?" I responded that I didn't. He told me that the larger one just has more zeros, explaining that the crime was the same, it was just more paper work. As I was tired of the undercover work, I agreed to accept the transfer.

IN October I started working in CCS. The first few months I worked on bankruptcy files and a few smaller fraud files. Then I was assigned to work with another member on an investment scheme investigation where the financial planner was an elder in his church, who was approached by a gentleman proposing a limited partnership investment plan that offered a higher rate of return than mutual funds. The financial planner agreed to speak to his clients and encouraged them to invest in this partnership.

Since most of the financial planner's clients knew him from the church and trusted him, they agreed to invest in this partnership. So the financial planner transferred their funds from mutual funds into the partnership

---

17   Commercial Crime Section also known as the fraud section

plan. Approximately $1.3 million was reinvested into the partnership plan.

From the start, the investments were paying a high rate of return, as a result many of the investors reinvested into other partnership plans that were being offered. But it turned out that the funds from one partnership were paying the high rate of returns in another plan. In the end, there were six individual plans that were using the funds from each other to pay the investors. Eventually, of course, the funds stopped coming in and their returns disappeared.

The investors wanted out of the plan and wanted their money back. When the financial planner couldn't get their money back, the investors came to our office to file a complaint. We took statements from each of the investors and the financial planner, I prepared search warrants on the financial institute and we reviewed all the banking information. It was clear the funds had been transferred to London, England into the banking institutions there, so I completed search warrants for those banking institutions as well. Once those warrants were approved, my partner and I flew to London, where we planned to interview the bankers who'd received the funds from Canada.

Upon our arrival, the English police officers advised us that all but one bank were refusing to speak to us. That was very disappointing, as we needed to follow the money trail, our records indicating that the funds were transferred from England to Switzerland and on to the Caymans. The one bank manager who did agree to talk to us advised the funds were indeed transferred to his bank, but that they were transferred back the very same day. The other documents that we brought to show him stated otherwise, but he insisted they were fake letters and forged statements.

All this is to say we learned the funds were ultimately transferred back into the suspect's personal bank account and used to purchase a house on Lakeshore Road in Oakville. Disappointingly, for our investigation, the suspect was arrested by the FBI first and spent two years in jail in the United States. Upon his return to Canada, we placed him under arrest, but by that point he'd declared bankruptcy and all the funds were gone.

Fraud is not considered a serious crime in Canada. In most cases, the judge blames the victims for being greedy and looking to make big gains. Whereas in my experience, I saw examples where elderly women had trusted their financial advisors to look after their affairs and were not being greedy at all. The consequences for these victims were far greater than the punishments for their crooked advisers, sentences involving little to no jail time and no restitution.

There was nothing I could do to help the victims in this case. Many were forced to sell their houses, others forced to return to work to help make ends meet. It was the saddest case I had worked on.

WORKING in the Fraud Section was very frustrating for me. I hated how long it took to work on a file. Getting banking records was slow, and writing a search warrant is time consuming and lenghty. Then, often the banks wouldn't get the banking records to you on time and you'd have to write another warrant. Banks were also not always helpful in handing over their records. In drug cases the arrests came fast, in frauds they took forever.

Even when you did get a conviction, the suspect just got house arrest and didn't even have to pay back any of the money. There seemed to be no justice for the victims and the pace of the work was agonizingly slow. To be fair, I had just come from the fast and exciting work of the Drug Section where doors were knocked down and people were arrested, just like on TV.

By the end of my first year in the Fraud Section, I started to drink on Sunday nights knowing I would have to spend another week at my desk hearing terrible stories about innocent people losing their money and realizing that all of my efforts wouldn't make things better for them.

*

MY last case while I was in the Fraud Section involved an identification theft as well as fraud. Identity theft was a huge problem in the United States, but something new in Canada.

I received a call from the head of the local newspaper agency stating that they had received several complaints from the local papers in the Hamilton area about a man and woman who were advertising "work from home" jobs in the local newspapers. The papers received the request to place these ads and were paid by cheque. The ads were printed in the paper, but it seemed the cheques had bounced. The agency wanted the RCMP to investigate the fraud.

These cheques were coming from areas in western Canada, and at first, my boss told me to hand this file over to the Hamilton Wentworth Regional Police Fraud Section since the frauds were taking place in the Hamilton area. I convinced him, though, that there was more to this fraud and that it involved other provinces. It appeared that these two suspects had been committing the same fraud across Canada and into the United States. They'd started this in BC, then Alberta, Saskatchewan, Manitoba and had now come to Ontario, and, to my surprise, Hamilton. While he agreed to let me keep the file, he still wanted the local police Fraud Section involved.

At the beginning of their scam, as I mentioned, the suspects would place the job ad in the paper, which then required job applicants to complete a form. Once they received the completed application forms showing a person's Social Insurance Number, mother's maiden name and date of birth, the couple would go a local government agency and report the identification lost or stolen in order to get replacement identification, but with their own photos on it. With the new identification in hand, the couple would open a bank account in that name, deposit a small amount of money and start writing cheques.

Those cheques would then be used to place more ads in the newspaper of the next town or city they were headed to and to purchase items they wanted. The account would at last run dry and the cheques would bounce.

This fraud was so tricky that when the police arrested a woman in Alberta for fraud, they arrested the real person, not the person who'd actually stolen her identity. Fortunately, I was able to locate a Global News story out of British Columbia about this scam featuring pictures of the two alleged fraudsters. I contacted the reporter and told her the suspects were now writing the same cheques in Ontario and was able to obtain her permission to use the story because we needed the photos of the actual suspects.

Having provided the Hamilton Wentworth Police Fraud Section with the pictures, they sent them to the local bank and put out a lookout for these two suspects. Within a day, the bank phoned to report the male suspect was at their branch. The police were dispatched and the man was apprehended. When I received the phone call that the male had been arrested, I started cheering so loudly that my boss walked down the hall to see what was going on.

There I was standing between two desks, one phone to one ear and another phone to the other, and told him, "We got them!" I couldn't believe we'd caught them. My boss smiled and gave me a thumbs up. That smile made it all worthwhile.

Later that same day, the female suspect was also arrested. I'd obtained a search warrant and executed it that night. In their apartment, we found additional fake identification and a pile of applications they could have gotten hundreds of further fake identifications with. Catching them was one of the best feelings in the world! They faced over a hundred fraud-related charges, and this case restored my hope that some fraudsters do go to jail.

IN December 1997, I volunteered to do Red Serge duties. One of my events was at Copps Coliseum in Hamilton at the Canadian Figure Skating Championships. Upon my arrival, I was asked if I could escort Barbara Ann Scott. I happily agreed. While we were sitting in the seats, a woman in front of me was startled and let out a scream. She shouted that a hand had reached out from underneath her and tried to steal her purse.

Dressed in full Red Serge, I got up and started running to get to the area where the hand had appeared. This required running up several flights of stairs, then running down a few more flights. Arriving at the back of the coliseum, I started looking under the stairs and there we found a man with a wallet in his hand. I placed him under arrest, put him in handcuffs, and escorted him to the security office. Once there we asked security to call the Hamilton Wentworth Police.

While waiting for the police to come and get the suspect, I looked into the wallet. Having located the name of the person whom the wallet belonged to, I asked security to make an announcement over the PA system asking the wallet's owner to come to the security office. When I handed her back her wallet, she was surprised as she hadn't even realized it was missing.

Some days, even on Red Serge duty, there was never a dull moment. I must have made quite a sight, running through the arena in my bright red RCMP uniform chasing down a pickpocket.

Chapter Thirty-Two

🍁

DURING THIS TIME, I WAS given some very special opportunities. I'd been attending a lot of events in my Red Serge, and doing a lot of volunteer work, becoming involved with the St. Leonard's Society, the Elizabeth Fry Society, and acting as a liaison officer with the Six Nations. Never having had a chance to do this much community work before, it became a passion for me, and over the course of my career, I've volunteered and participated in many different charity events, serving as the coordinator for the Terry Fox Run, the Special Olympics Torch Run and the United Way, to name a few.

I also signed up for the Cops for Cancer event. Having my hair shaved off to raise funds for cancer didn't seem like a big deal. Some people sponsored me to shave my hair off, and others offered me money to NOT do it! It was a very humbling experience, though. My hairdresser not only cut all my hair off, he took a razor and cleaned it right off. I received a lot of stares and raised a lot of money.

Soon after the event, I saw myself in the mirror one day and thought, *I look like a cancer patient.* It gave me a bit of an insight into how they must feel when people stare at their bald heads—people making comments about your hair, just staring, or even walking away from you because they think you're a skinhead. The one thing I learned for sure was how cold it felt without hair. At night, I had to sleep with a cap on my head since otherwise I'd get rashes from rubbing against the pillow, and it always felt like a cool breeze was blowing on the top of my head.

I ended up shaving my hair off three more times for different charities. For the last one, when they asked me to shave my head again, I told them that was getting boring so I added a twist. We sold tickets at two dollars each, and the winning ticket could pick out the colour that I would dye my hair, wearing it that colour for a week before I shaved it off. Well, ultimately, the joke really was on me.

The winner chose the colour green—a nice deep forest green. I didn't think anything of it, until the next day when my pillowcase was green. My bed sheets were green. The collars of my shirts were green and every time I took a shower the water turned green.

By the end of the week my hair was a bright neon green colour, and when it came time to shave my hair off, the clippers got stuck in my hair and wouldn't cut. Some of my friends sat me down and used scissors, cutting off as much as they could. Then I jumped in the shower and shaved the rest off. I never did it again.

LITTLE did I know at the time, that my boss was taking notice of all my volunteer work and nominated me up for a national award. Although I didn't win, people in senior management had heard about me. Then during a conference in Cornwall, the Commanding Officer of Ontario approached me, telling me he thought I had what it takes to become a Commissioned Officer [18] and he wanted to help me get there. I was caught off guard, but very pleased.

He wanted me to accept a transfer to the Training Section so that I

---

18   RCMP regular members who have been appointed to the rank of Inspector and above

could round out my career with some administrative experience, suggesting I stay in Training for a couple of years, and then get back into policing again. I must admit, for the first time in my life, I had a big head. I thought I was something special because he picked me—*ME*—and wanted to help advance my career.

Then he asked me to organize a major conference for all the senior managers in Niagara Falls, another request that felt like a major honour. Of course, like all good things, it was four to six months before anything happened.

*

WHILE I was waiting for things to progress, my head shrank back down to its regular size, but my excitement continued to grow. And finally, in May of 1999, I was transferred to O Division Training Section. It felt like a dream come true!

As a young girl I'd sometimes pictured myself as a teacher, but ultimately followed my dream of becoming an RCMP officer. Now here I was in the training branch about to realize both of them. I had never expected this. I know that many people never get to reach their goals, but here I was being told it *was* possible to have my cake and eat it too!

Chapter Thirty-Three

🍁

THE TRAINING SECTION ONCE HAD ten members assigned to it and it was now down to just two. I would learn that when money is tight in the RCMP, Training is the first place that cuts funds. At first, the Training Section members were very resentful about my arrival. While most were packing up their stuff to move to a new section, here I was moving in. To them it seemed unfair.

Also, I was permitted to stay in Hamilton and commute to London and other areas in Ontario. That pissed off a few more people because that meant I needed a car to drive around in, and that one would be assigned to me. Not everyone was given that privilege.

In time, I was assigned a marked RCMP cruiser. I initially thought they'd given me that car on purpose to make me uncomfortable since I'd upset a lot of people and maybe this was one way to get even. I didn't care. I had a way to get to the work sites and get to the job at hand. I was too excited to be in the Training Section to let their attitudes get me down.

Imagine what it feels like to drive an RCMP cruiser for the first time. I recalled the comment I'd made so many years earlier in New Brunswick to the officer who let me sit in his car. Here I was in the *front*, not the back, of my very own cruiser!

The first night I drove the cruiser home, my next-door neighbours came out to look at it and their son, sitting in the front, began hitting the buttons. The next thing I knew, he had the lights and sirens going. Once I'd figured out which buttons he'd pushed—there was no teaching manual with the car—I was able to shut them off.

On the back of the driver's seat was a rifle rack. Somehow the boy had also opened the rack, so I used my right hand to reach back to close it. Then suddenly my fingers were caught in the rack. I thought I might have broken my fingers. Of course, I didn't let on that my hand was stuck.

Once the neighbours left, I had to figure out which button would release the rack. Well, that was harder than expected, as I had to reach over with my left hand to try and find the button. I eventually did find the right button and released my fingers. There they were, four very flat fingers. The good news was they weren't broken, just very sore. I'd need to learn fast how that control panel worked.

IN addition to the resentment from the other officers, driving the marked cruiser turned out to have another issue. Every time I drove it down the highway, it would look like I was leading a parade. No one would pass me.

Cars would zoom up beside me, and as soon as they saw the words POLICE, they would slow down, drive in my blind spot, then fall back behind me. I'm sure many drivers cursed me because I certainly didn't want to speed while driving in a marked police car. When I mentioned this issue to the Transportation Section, they suggested they could get a sign that stated "Not in Service", like a bus, but I didn't like that idea so agreed to drive it the way it was.

AS I continued to use this marked car to get myself to and from work, other issues continued to crop up that were not my responsibility. For instance, people whose cars had broken down or had accidents would wave me down. People would see the car and assume that you were there to help them. Naturally, I would stop to help, and after a while, I even started wearing my uniform, since it made it easier to carry my equipment, in case I would need it, instead of in my purse or briefcase.

One day, a vehicle entered the highway at a high rate of speed, and another driver, catching my eye, gave me a look as if to say, "What are you going to do about that?" So I turned on my emergency lights, caught up to car and made it pull over.

You must understand that I do not have any authority under the *Highway Traffic Act*. This was in no way part of my responsibilities. But I felt it looked bad to other drivers if I just ignored it, so I called the OPP to have a cruiser dispatched to our location. There were four men in the car and I told them to stay in the vehicle because another cruiser was on the way. Twenty minutes later, the OPP arrived.

I explained what had happened, and the OPP asked how fast the car was going. As I didn't have radar in the car, I told the officer that I'd been going at least 140 km/h before the car pulled over. The driver admitted to driving 140 km/h, and also confessed that they were police foundations students on their way to school. As the OPP issued him a speeding ticket for driving 40 km/h over the speed limit, I told the driver that he'd have a great story to tell his instructor about why he was late for class.

I was then asked by the OPP officer to have my car's speedometer calibrated and to submit a statement in case this went to court! That was the first and only speeding ticket I was involved with enforcing.

ONE day, as I was driving to London, I observed an OPP cruiser driving up beside me. It slowed down, the officer waved at me, then accelerated away at a higher rate of speed. After that, I got the idea that driving at 120 km/h instead of 100 would end the parades. But no, it did not. At one point, I considered rolling down my window and waving the cars on to pass me, but then I thought that if the OPP caught them speeding, they'd they tell the officer that an RCMP officer waved them on. So I decided I would just keep leading the parades.

IN August 1999, at the request of the Commanding Officer, I was assigned to assist the Hamilton Wentworth Police at the Chief of Policing Conference. He wanted me to learn about hosting a conference, as I would be organizing the Commanding Officers Conference. I attended the planning meeting and made notes that would assist me.

During the conference, the organizers asked me to be a greeter at the entrance because I was bilingual and could assist with any French-speaking members. I asked that a sign be made that read, "Je Parle Français", that way the French-speaking delegates would see the sign and could ask me for directions in French. To my amusement, I kept getting called Francis.

For a moment, I didn't get it. Then it dawned on me that they thought the sign was my name tag and that Francais was my name. I got nicknamed "Francis the Wal-Mart greeter"! The name stuck!

Regrettably, the Commanding Officers Conference was cancelled.

WHILE posted in Training Section, I was provided with many opportunities to obtain training myself and then teach the new skills I had learned. Unfortunately, many of the courses I taught were not as successful as I first thought they'd be. Becoming an instructor for a course called Interest Based Negotiations, it was hoped that by providing supervisors with some negotiation skills, it would allow them to work better with their employees. Like many courses, there was a lot of theory, but no practical application, which did not prove successful. Following that, we gave them the Advanced Negotiation course with similar results.

Eventually, some of us who'd trained under these two courses became negotiators and tried to resolve issues between employees under the ADR[19] Program. It seemed that the ADR Program had become more of a "How much will it cost to make this go away?" program and was cancelled in the end. All ADR decisions were sealed and a confidentially agreement signed by all parties. This is how we dealt with situations—we covered them up and made sure no one would talk about them again.

THEN we also had Covey Leadership Training. At first, only senior management was offered this training. Although the RCMP sent members to Covey to become trained as instructors, on my very first course, a senior officer told the group that he was forced to take this course despite the fact he was retiring. Covey training lasted about three to four years before the RCMP dropped it.

We also trained members to become First Aid and CPR instructors, who would then travel around the Division and train our members. Within a few years, though, the RCMP dropped this, as they didn't want to pay to have instructors recertified. Then we also had members trained to teach the boating course. That too ended up being dropped. And the Employees Continuous Development Program, which RCMP supervisors were also trained in, was dropped within four to five years for the Bridging the Gap Program.

The RCMP was trying to keep pace with changing legislation and policies by using a variety of training, and it appeared that whenever the RCMP received bad press or bad case law, training was usually seen as the solution to the problem. Dishearteningly, we would train someone to become an expert in one area, only to see that person get promoted to a different area. Or, we would offer a course on counterfeiting to a section

19   Alternative Dispute Resolution

that already had ten people trained in it, but wanted everyone in their section to be trained.

There is only so much money to go around, and when budgets are being cut, the training budget is one of the first to go. The greatest cost for training is the administrative costs—travel, hotel and meals making up the majority of it. The RCMP didn't have a training centre in Ontario, so we had to get quotes for local hotels to include conference rooms and accommodations. Even though the RCMP does have the training Depot in Regina, the travel cost to bring in members from across the country is very high.

I truly believe in the importance of training, but in my role as trainer, I'd see other problems besides a lack of training. For example, when we were offering a course, the detachment commander would be advised that a training course was coming up and told how many positions they were allotted on that course. Then they would submit the names of their candidates. Once the course would start, it would become very obvious to us as trainers which employees had asked to go on the course, which were told to go on the course, and who was there to get a holiday.

Chapter Thirty-Four

🍁

EVENTUALLY, I WAS ISSUED AN unmarked car to get around to my training assignments. This happened during a period of budget trimming, and the Commanding Officer at the time had told the Transportation section to purchase smaller cars that would be more economical on gas. Mine was a bluish, purple Neon. I called it the Barney-Mobile because it was the same colour as the children's TV character Barney. Others called it the Smarties car, but in any case, it seemed a sad excuse for a police cruiser—not the image I'd been hoping to project.

Ultimately, however, it would seem that Karma played a role in my transportation situation.

Sadly, a Mountie in British Columbia was killed in a motor vehicle accident, and because he was originally from Brantford, the regimental funeral was being held in there. Dressed in my Red Serge, I attended the funeral, but before the end of the service, the officer in charge of the Hamilton/Niagara Detachment asked me if I could drive the Commissioner to the Brantford airport. I reluctantly agreed.

Not only was the car a source of embarrassment for me, but I had driven it recently with my dog in the back seat. So I planned to put the Commissioner in the front seat with me and his luggage in the trunk. No problem.

I drove to the Best Western Hotel to pick up the Commissioner. When his assistant came out, I informed him that I was there to drive the Commissioner to the airport. He then grabbed some luggage and followed me to the car. Opening the trunk, he placed the luggage inside, and few minutes later, the Commissioner came out and his assistant pointed to my car. The Commissioner looked at the car and asked, "Is that a Police cruiser"?

I stated, "Yes, sir!"

He looked annoyed, but walked toward the car, opened the back door and sat down. All I could think of was all the dog hair in the back seat. His assistant sat in the front and I drove them to the airport. The Commissioner never speaking a word to me.

When we arrived at the airport, though, he got out of the car and yelled, "Have you had a dog or cat in the back of this car?"

"Yes, sir," I replied. "I did."

"There's hair all over my boot bag!"

Luckily, I had a lint brush and handed it to him. He wiped down his boot bag, but he was so mad that he was shaking. And I kept thinking that I was in big trouble. But thankfully, we don't wear a nametag on our Red Serge uniforms and I hadn't introduced myself.

As he headed to the plane, I decided not to tell the Commissioner he was covered with dog hair all along the back of his clothes. He would *not* be happy with me when he got home and discovered this for himself.

Returning to London, I told the Transportation section manager what had happened and she started to laugh. She told me that he was the one who'd made her buy the Neons and thought it was Karma that he had been forced to drive in one!

ANOTHER interesting experience happened to me another time when I was volunteering to do Red Serge duties at Copps Coliseum during the Canadian Figure Skating Championships. Elvis Stojko, the reigning men's champion, approached me and asked why the RCMP always looked so serious when they are working. I told him that was the way we were trained.

Elvis then asked me, "When I come out to do my program, will you smile at me if I salute you?" and then saluted me the American way.

"Yes," I answered, "I'll smile if you salute me the Mountie way." The RCMP is the only Canadian police service that still salutes the British way.

Elvis agreed to learn, so I showed him how to properly salute in the RCMP—"Long way up, short way down" with your palm facing outward. Elvis practised a couple of times, and we agreed to salute and smile when he came back out to do his program.

Then Elvis also asked me if I would help him play a joke on Shae Lynn Bourne and Victor Kraatz, explaining that during the last winter Olympics, Bourne and Kraatz had been caught trying to smuggle an Olympic flag inside their suitcase. He wanted me to pretend the reason I was there was to investigate that incident. Laughing, I agreed to play along.

During practice, Bourne and Kraatz were sitting on the bench getting ready to skate when I approached them with a serious face and asked if they were Bourne and Kraatz, which they said they were. I explained that I was there to investigate a complaint for the International Olympic Association about an attempted theft of an Olympic flag.

The looks on their faces were priceless, but after a few seconds, I couldn't help it, I started to laugh!

"Did Elvis ask you to do this?" they asked.

I nodded as I continued to laugh. What a jokester that Elvis Stojko is!

When it was Elvis' time to skate, I came to attention, he saluted me the Mountie way and I smiled at him. Little did I know that ABC Sports had caught the moment on live TV.

I did a lot of Red Serge duties during this time in my career. Most members in my detachment avoided them—one member would even pay $20 for someone else to take his turn at Red Serge details—but I loved doing it.

One time, I was the coordinator for the Old Timers Hockey game, which was where the NHL Old Timers would play a hockey game against the Law Enforcement team. A portion of the ticket sales for the game would be donated to the charity of our choice, and as the coordinator, I got to pick the charity. Once, I picked Parkinson's as a member in Niagara Detachment had advanced Parkinson's. Another time, I picked the Hamilton Cancer Clinic, since my best friend's mother had cancer and was getting her treatments there.

During that hockey game, I was wearing my Red Serge and standing with my friend's mom, waiting to go into the dressing room to see the NHL Old Timers players. We were chatting with Bobby Hall, when two ladies walked past us and into the change room.

My friend's mom asked, "Hey, why can't we get in?"

So I looked at Bobby Hall and he said, "Okay, you two can go in."

We walked into the change room at the exact same moment that Mark Napier was walking out of the showers completely naked. I turned away quickly, but my friend's mom got the full picture!

Of course, Mark Napier was not happy, and the next thing I knew everyone was told to get out of the change room until the players were ready. My friend's mom wanted to wait and go back in, but I said, "You can, but I can't. I am the only RCMP officer in Red Serge and Mark Napier saw me. I can't go back in until I change into my regular clothes."

And that is what I did. It saved both Napier and me the embarrassment of meeting again.

MEMBERS of the RCMP are generally held up as role models for children, but sometimes this would get me in trouble through no fault of my own. One time, I'd brought back lobster for my friends in Niagara. On the night we ate the lobster, I told my friends that the shape of the brain of the lobster looked like the Virgin Mary praying. I cracked open the shell, took out the brain, and showed them the resemblance.

The next day, my friend got a call from his ten-year-old son's school. Apparently, his son had misunderstood me, and was telling the kids in his class that I'd told his family the brain of the lobster looked like a *vagina*.

On another occasion, I was telling friends, a husband and wife, about the time I was standing on the street corner posing as a prostitute. Sometime later, the wife asked if I would go and speak to the students at her daughter Danielle's school. So there I was, standing at the front of the class in my Red Serge, and the first question I was asked was, "Tell me about the time you were a stripper?"

Of course, I was a bit confused by the question and responded that I was never a stripper. I continued on with my presentation and another student asked me the same question. Once again, I clarified that I'd never been a stripper. Then one of the students said, "Well, Danielle told us you were a stripper!"

Danielle had misunderstood my conversation with her parents about my undercover work and I was never able to convince those students that I hadn't been a stripper!

Chapter Thirty-Five

🍁

DURING A TRAINING CONFERENCE IN Toronto for the International Association of Women in Policing, the RCMP had requested that all the RCMP officers attending the conference get together for a meet-and-greet. Five of the most senior female officers were in attendance, one of whom stated that women had the KSA—Knowledge Skills and Abilities—to succeed in the RCMP.

Having raised my hand, she allowed me to speak. I suggested that she was missing an A—I felt it should be Knowledge Skills Abilities and *Attitude*, since it was our attitudes that allowed women to succeed.

Later when the session was over, that senior officer approached me and offered to be my mentor if I should want to enter into the Officer Program.

THE turnover rate for women in policing must be very high.

When I was first stationed in Niagara in 1987, the Niagara Police Service had thirty female officers. In 1996, when I left, they had thirty-five. At some point, in order to improve their numbers, the Niagara Police were recruiting older women who'd already had children. It appeared that, although women left the force for a wide variety of reasons, many women leave policing when they have children.

After I'd arrived in Hamilton, an officer from Hamilton who was involved with Ontario Women in Law Enforcement asked me what the highest rank of a female in the RCMP in Ontario was. Telling her it was the rank of corporal, she clarified her question by stating that she'd not just meant in the Hamilton Detachment, but in the entire province of Ontario. I had to tell her I'd understood her question, but that the answer was the same. She was stunned.

The Deputy Police Chief in Niagara was the same woman whom I worked with to learn to buy drugs. In just over six years with the OPP, she'd gone from a constable to the Deputy Chief. Whereas with the RCMP, I was still a constable.

And later, when I later taught at the Ontario Police College, the average was only four women in every group of twenty-four cadets. Although the RCMP has said it wants to increase the percentage of women, I'm not sure how successful they have been.

WHILE I was posted in Training Section, I applied to St. Francis Xavier University to complete a certificate in Adult Education, which I completed in July 2000. One of the most important things I learned on this course were the three Vs of training.

Each training course had three types of students. The first V was the Volunteer. They wanted to be there, wanted to learn. They make the best students.

The second V was the victim. That person was told to take the training and didn't want to be there. They were the tough students.

The last V was the Vacationer. That student would disrupt the class or just totally not participate. Later it was called the three Ps—The Participant, The Prisoner and The Partygoer. Regardless of which you called it, this training would pay off for me in a few years.

IN April 2001, I was assigned to work the Summit of the Americas in Quebec City. My job was to escort the luggage of the delegates from the airport to the hotels where they would be staying.

One of the most amazing things I saw was when Air Force One landed. What a huge plane! And when President Bush and his wife walked out the door of the plane, they looked so small against it.

When American presidents visit another country, everything they need is brought them inside Air Force One. As the front of the plane started to lift up and opened, I saw the president's limo, helicopters, and escort vehicles emerging from inside the plane. The Americans also bring with them all their own food and water, and when a meal is prepared for the president, a member of the Secret Service will watch the food being made and stay with that plate until it's served to the president.

At this summit, there were huge protests, beginning with about 20,000 demonstrators, some wearing hockey gear for protection. On the first day the barricades came down and the protestors took over the streets, there were riots and a lot of violence. As we waited at the airport, we saw the TV coverage of the protesters, the news reports estimating that the number of people marching was anywhere from 50,000 to 150,000. The Emergency Response Teams, who were also waiting at the airport, were deployed at last and had been given tear gas to deal with the violence.

As we were heading toward the hotels and toward the riots, the protesters surrounded my vehicle and I knew we had to get out of that situation. I was working with a very junior member, so I told him to stay in the car while I got out and ordered the crowd to move, then got back in the car and started to edge forward. Luckily, the crowd moved and we were able to get away from that area.

Seeing the protestors dressed in camouflage outfits, wearing hockey equipment, and carrying slingshots was a menacing sight. You ask yourself, *Why would protesters would dress up like that? Were they* looking *for trouble?*

Finally entering the secure zone, we were exposed to tear gas, but didn't have gas masks. Unfortunately, the tear gas was deployed into the wind, which then blew it toward the hotels instead of the protesters. In fact, so much tear gas was deployed that we had to order in more from the United States. As well, the tear gas ended up entering the ventilation systems of some of the hotels and they were forced to evacuate and throw out all of the contaminated food.

At night, we drove around the city and saw the protesters huddled under bridges, standing around fires to stay warm, just waiting to regroup and protest again. It was quite something to see and experience—like out of a TV show. The next day, we were issued with gas masks, but told not to use them unless it was necessary since were informed that the gas mask canisters cost $70 each.

As it turned out though, fans—the kinds used on ski resorts—were placed along the perimeter to try to disperse the tear gas and direct it away from the secure zone.

The next day, the newspapers featured a story that appeared to show police brutality, a protestor covered in red around his head and face. What the press had failed to realize was that the protester had taken a balloon filled with red paint and smashed it against his head to make it look like he'd been beaten. It's amazing how a story can be taken out of context. It was a hoax that became front-page news. Nevertheless, the violence was real and this was the most violent event I'd ever worked at.

Chapter Thirty-Six

🍁

I TOOK FULL ADVANTAGE OF the opportunities training allowed me, and from May 15 to 31, 2001, I attended the Public and Police Safety Instructors course in Cornwall, Ontario. Housed at the Nav Can Training Centre, there were thirty candidates, twenty-eight men and two women, counting me. Several of the males on the course were from our Emergency Response Team. To my knowledge we were the first two females to be trained as instructors in O Division.

During one training session on Use of Force, a male threw his hockey protection cup at me and said, "Here is your facemask." He did this in front of all the candidates.

I picked up his cup, looked at it and then asked, "Were you injured? It's so small!" Everybody laughed and he never teased me again, but it was another example of how female members could never let their guard down, as more harassment was always just around the corner.

I had always been told that the best defence was a good offence. Many times, during work or training, I had to "prove myself" to the guys. Fortunately, that was always easy for me, as I love hard work. I'd waited for my opportunity to be an officer and nothing or no one was going to take it away from me without a fight.

I decided to become a Use of Force Instructor. At the end of the course, the lead instructor approached me. He was so impressed by my skills and ability to teach, that he asked me to become an instructor on the next PPSI[20] course. He explained how there was a mistaken belief that you had to be 6'2" and a man to teach Use of Force Training. He wanted a female in the program to counter this belief and he liked the way I handled myself.

As a result, I taught on the next PPSI course held in Cornwall and also on the course after that held in Fredericton, New Brunswick. Of course, as an instructor, I was expected to hang out with the other instructors and not the candidates. Inevitably, that always involved drinking, and when the guys are drinking the conversation always turned to inappropriate topics, such as asking me about my sex life. It never seemed to end.

At one point, the lead instructor asked me to travel out to British Columbia for another course, but my supervisor stepped in and said I couldn't as we had only three trainers in O Division and they could not afford for me to be away from my regular duties. In many ways, I was relieved.

Being the only female instructor was hard enough without getting questioned about my personal life. Thankfully, I like sports and could handle the conversations about sports, but every now and again most girls crave a conversation that doesn't involve sports or sex. That part of my job still felt the same as it had that first day I arrived in Niagara. I was still the only girl in a man's world.

One of the best coping skills I had was physical fitness. Working in a high stress area such as drugs and working in a male-dominated work environment, I found running and weight training as my relief. Knowing how important it is in law enforcement to be in good physical condition, I

---

20   Public and Police Officer Safety Instructor formally known as the Use of Force Instructor

took this very seriously. And because I'm small, I knew that my life and the lives of my coworkers and the public could be at stake. I also knew that the most important skill in law enforcement isn't just being fit, it's being smart!

As a woman, I felt I had to outwit, outsmart and outwork some of my male colleagues, which wasn't always difficult to do, but it became tiresome. Always having to be prepared with a come back to a disrespectful comment or gesture, always having to prove myself.

IN 2002, I was responsible for the Cadet Field Coaching Program in "O" Division, training the Field Coaches, receiving their progress reports, and once they had successfully completed their training, ensuring that the new members would receive their increase in pay. Later, the new members were sent to other police services in Ontario so that they could get a taste of uniform policing.

Since the mandate of the RCMP had changed to Organized Crime, Terrorism and National and International Drug Investigations, it became harder and harder to get experience testifying in court. The hope was that, by working with the local police forces, those opportunities would come, and once it was determined that the local police would be training our new members, then I would meet with them to ensure they understood our program.

I organized a tour of the RCMP academy for the Niagara Regional Police and Brantford Police Coaching Officer. We toured Depot in Regina for three days to show them what our training was like. During the tour, an officer from Niagara remarked she hadn't realize how many electric cars there were in Regina, pointing to the electrical outlets we used to plug in the car. These were used for the block heaters in the cars. I explained to her that it got so cold there in the winter that if you turned off the car, it would not start again because the oil would freeze. Of course, being from southern Ontario, she had no idea that this could happen.

Regrettably, having our recruits trained by another agency had its share of challenges. During this timeframe, the RCMP was the only police service that didn't have to submit a report if they took out their service pistols, and it was rumoured that some of the Ontario police services would make the RCMP cadets go into a dangerous call first because they could take their pistols out and not have to submit reports.

I decided to address that issue and advised the field coaches and cadets that if the Ontario police services don't go in at the same time as the RCMP officers, the RCMP officers were not to go in alone. Officer safety is paramount. If you need to write a report, WRITE THE REPORT!

Chapter Thirty-Seven

🍁

IN 2002, I WAS PROMOTED to the rank of corporal. What should have been a happy day turned into one of the saddest days of my life since that was the same day I had to put my dog down.

I'd have given back the promotion to keep my dog.

EVENTUALLY, the RCMP decided to downsize responsibility by adding another layer of authority. We got rid of divisions and added regions. I was a member of O Division training which then became part of Central Region Training.

Under this new structure, the three members in O Division responsible for the training of 1,200 members in Ontario became part of a fifteen-person training team responsible for training of 4,000 to 5,000 in Ontario and Quebec. On paper it looked like a great idea, but in reality, my supervisor was posted in Ottawa and I was in London, so for me it meant a lot more travelling. I was called upon to help teach the new members of Training Section in both Montreal and Ottawa, and as the subject matter expert in the Employees Continuous Development Program and Cadet Field Coaching Program, I was asked to share this knowledge.

Then it was decided to centralize certain job functions, with the boss assigning a member in Ottawa to be responsible for the Cadet Field

Program in Central Region, who would be tasked to travel and look after all the new members arriving from Depot. I wasn't thrilled about these changes as I had created the program and now it was being taken away from me.

And then Learning and Development Branch at National Headquarters decided that the Employees Continuous Development Program wasn't working and wanted to develop a new program, so I was asked to come to Ottawa and help create the new program. The issue was, the person from Learning and Development with whom I was asked to work didn't want to make any changes to the current program. In the end, though, the bosses in Ottawa agreed with the changes I wanted to make and asked me to transfer to Ottawa to implement the new program. As a result, I was transferred in August 2003 to Headquarters in Ottawa to work on a project called *Bridging the Gap* (BTG). BTG is a performance improvement process which would identify areas where there is a need to improvement performance for both the section and individual members.

This relocation to Ottawa was extremely stressful for me, as the member who had raped me was stationed there, and even just being in Ottawa brought back the memories of the sexual assault that I had suppressed. I couldn't deal with them, so I started drinking more and more.

Although I was lucky enough to stay at a friend's house with her and her family for the first three months, ultimately, I was moved into a hotel and I spent a lot of time alone and was in fact very lonely in Ottawa. For the next two and a half years, I lived out of hotel rooms. At night, everyone went home and I went back to an empty hotel room.

I travelled extensively throughout Ontario, Quebec and Alberta, but during the first two to three months, I worked in Ottawa and would drive home to Brantford on Friday evening and then drive back to Ottawa on Sunday nights. I needed to be home where I felt safe. It became so unbearable I began to count the number of days I'd have to serve to reach twenty years of service. I wanted out.

IN November 2003, I held the first Train the Trainer session. In attendance were the Training and Staffing personnel from every division. I later found out that many of the candidates had no idea why they were in attendance and that they didn't even understand they were expected to teach this material back in their own divisions. Finally, a person from Staffing asked, "What if the member refuses to complete a Performance Agreement?" I didn't have an answer to his question.

Then the officer in charge of Learning and Development stood up and in a loud angry voice said, "Breau, answer the question!" I tried my best to provide an answer but I was so embarrassed.

At the end of the session, my boss came in and, still upset, told me that had better not ever happen again. I was tired, hurt and then angry. I'd given up my time, energy and placed myself in a very stressful situation and this is what I get in return.

I told him to find someone else to do his dirty work. Then a private consultant stood up against him and told him that he thought I was the only person who could pull this off, and that he had better back off.

The next day, my boss apologized and we continued the sessions, but I felt more than ever that I had taken on a job situation I was not able to cope with. The job was for a two-year commitment, and there was no one else willing to take it on.

OVER time, I started to drink earlier and earlier at home to help me deal with my anger and anxiety. I knew something was wrong with me, so I went to my family doctor and told him I thought I was going through PMS. I told him about my anger.

He put me on birth control pills, but they didn't help. It wasn't until I started having anxiety attacks that I told my family doctor that I was depressed and he put me on antidepressants. At first, they didn't help and he had to increase the dosage until he could get it regulated.

Eventually, I needed sleeping pills to go to sleep. I knew that the mixture of antidepressants, sleeping pills and alcohol was dangerous but I couldn't find any other way to cope. At last, after three months of driving back and forth to Brantford, the RCMP agreed to let me fly home. I would fly home on Friday nights and back to Ottawa on Monday mornings.

AFTER the Train the Trainer sessions, I started travelling to each site in Ontario and Quebec, as well as sites in Alberta. The never-ending road show began. Each site required at least two to three visits. I had well over fifty sections in the process and more on the way. The Western Provinces were more receptive to the process as the membership was younger in age and in years of service, and they needed training. In fact, some detachments had all junior members and no senior members to coach and mentor them.

Conversely, in Ontario and Quebec, the average age of the membership was over fifty and the average service was thirty years. These were employees who were getting ready to retire and looking for a promotion to increase their pension upon retirement. They didn't want to do the process and resisted it as it was paper intensive, requiring a lot of work by both the members and their supervisors. Many claimed they didn't have the time to do this program. BTG was a very hard sell.

The constant traveling was brutal. When I'd joined the RCMP, I signed a declaration that I was willing to serve anywhere in Canada, but this was a bit extreme. One night, I went out for supper with a group after a BTG session, and when I stepped outside, I realized I didn't know which city or province I was in. I stopped and tried to remember where I was but couldn't.

I was struggling with all the travelling and stress I was under, and my drinking was getting out of control. I'd asked for a transfer back to Ontario, and at one point, I was offered a transfer back to Hamilton CCS—someone had been found who was willing to take over my training job—and I accepted. As the transfer got closer, I was called into the office of the superintendent in charge of BTG and was told that the person who was to take over my position had backed out. It turns out that she couldn't teach in French, which was a requirement, so I was told I couldn't go to Hamilton after all. My transfer was cancelled. I was very disappointed but pushed on.

Chapter Thirty-Eight

🍁

NEAR THE END OF MY time in Ottawa, I started having anxiety attacks when I was flying home for the weekends. Once the plane took off, I started feeling anxious and couldn't control the feeling that the plane was going to crash. I kept trying to tell myself that it was okay, but I couldn't shake the feeling.

When I slept, I would grind my teeth so badly, I woke up with terrible headaches. I was withdrawing from friends and family. I didn't want to leave the house after coming home for the weekends. My energy level dropped, and I wanted to go to bed early and earlier each night. The later into the evening, the more my anxiety level would rise, and I drank to calm myself down.

Every Monday, I would go to work all smiles, but after work I would take it out on my roommate. I wanted to hit, throw things and, at times, I did act out by kicking things and yelling. I'd get so anxious I felt like I was going to explode, both physically and mentally. I started taking shortcuts at work, and my supervisor called me in to discuss what I was doing and why I was taking shortcuts. I lost it and had a meltdown right in front of him. I told him I couldn't do this job anymore. I had given a two-year commitment and it was now in year three, and still no one would take over my job. No one wanted it. I was trapped and couldn't get out.

As a result of this, a transfer was arranged for me back to "O" Division. The course that I'd put together and trained other members to use is now mandatory for all newly promoted supervisors. I was proud to have this as my legacy, but the costs to bringing it about left me at the lowest point of my career.

*

IN 2006, I was transferred to RCMP Headquarters in London, being given a job as the Sensitive Expenditure Coordinator. This involved reviewing all expense claims made by undercover operators or expenses made during a policing operation involving undercover operations. Since the job had been vacant for some time, I had to train myself, but due to my undercover work experience, I already had some understanding of it. Within a week, however, the CROPS officer told me that I wouldn't be in this job long, as he wanted to downsize the position and move it to the financial expenses section. I didn't care at that point—I was just glad to be in one place for a while.

The work pace was very slow and there was not a lot of work, but I needed the break. I still couldn't talk about my work in Ottawa without crying, and to make matters even worse, the person that I'd worked with in Montreal Training Branch had a massive heart attack and died at the age of forty-seven, leaving behind a wife and nine-year-old girl. I blamed it all on the stress and travel we did on the Bridging the Gap project.

Within a couple of weeks in the new job, I found a lot of discrepancies in a high-profile section. Having put together a package, I made a presentation to the officers in charge that the section-in-question had made several expenditures that were not within the *Financial Administration Act*. Should this information get out to the press, it would be the end of this section. As this was a high-profile section, that was not an option, and this case ended up on the RCMP Commissioner's desk.

The longer I was in this job, the more problems I found. Most of the issues were related to signing authorities. Members who were no longer in the RCMP, or even who were suspended, still appeared on the list as having signing authority. I'd jokingly say that I hadn't found a dead member's name of the list yet, but it wouldn't be long!

Together with Financial Services, we suspended all signing authorities and had each manager complete a new form with their signature and an up-to-date list. Now, each time I received an expense claim, I could check to ensure the proper signatures were attached.

Another issue was the outstanding money advances to members who'd requested money to fund projects that were no longer active. One member had over $50,000 just sitting in his locker for over a year. How do you forget you have $50,000 sitting in your locker?

I ended up contacting the supervisor of each person who had an outstanding advance and requested the immediate return of the funds. At the same time, I was able to make improvements to prevent issues like that from happening again, and once I incorporated the changes, I had things running more smoothly.

As a result of the changes I had incorporated in "O" Division, the National Coordinator asked for permission to have me attend the reviews in J, H, and K Divisions. So I flew to New Brunswick, met the team and conducted a review at Headquarters in Fredericton. Then we drove to Halifax and conducted our review there. Next, we flew to Calgary for a review there, and finally drove to Edmonton for another one.

At the end of the reviews, I returned to my Division to submit my notes to the National Coordinator, who asked for me to come to Ottawa for a meeting between the RO 580 coordinators [21]from across the country. After the conference, I was asked to stay in Ottawa for an additional week, and there I was asked to review and rewrite the National Policy with another member from K division and the National RO Coordinator in Ottawa.

The new policy would implement all the changes that I had incorporated in my own Division, plus a few new things that we had identified during our reviews.

Several years later, the new National Policy was implemented. I found it extraordinary that I could be involved in the writing of a policy that would now be the way of doing business across the country. It was a humbling feeling. And it just goes to show, you don't have to be the boss to help make the RCMP better. Everyone can play a part. I feel blessed to have had several opportunities to help improve aspects of the RCMP such as this.

IN 2006, I was trained as an instructor for ethics. The first course had been put together by a professor from Berkley in the United States, and our feedback was that it would be very difficult to teach RCMP officers using American examples of corruption. We had enough examples of our own issues. This course was also slated to be a week long, and it would be challenging to hold a course for that long, especially one members think they didn't need.

That course was eventually dropped and I thought that would be the end of it, but within a year or two, I was contacted to attend yet another trainer course in ethics. This time, I was the only person, who had been trained in the first one, that returned for the second course.

The RCMP had conducted a study of cases across Canada, called Project Sanction, which proved to be a much better course, and came to

---

21   Regular members and Public Servants responsible for expenditures under the Financial code RO 580.

be used as part of the Supervisor/Leadership course. In the study, cases were collected from each division to determine ways in which RCMP employees had gone wrong, the top three areas where employees got into trouble being: theft or fraud, unauthorized use of a police computer, and discreditable conduct. The RCMP even had a website, containing all the cases where employees had been brought before an adjudication hearing because of their conduct.

Some of the cases on this site were unbelievable. There were hundreds of examples of shocking behaviour on the part of the RCMP and very little evidence of significant consequences. My exposure to this information really changed my attitude toward the institution, and there came a time when I was not so proud to tell people what I did for a living. Many of these stories were broadcast in the news during this time and the image of the RCMP took quite a public beating.

TEACHING ethics to police officers was not an easy sell. Most employees would say, "We know the difference between right and wrong. We don't need this training" or "Why don't you teach this to senior management?"

My response would be, "Why are we always on the front page of the news if we know right from wrong?"

One common example was that RCMP employees are not allowed to receive any favours or money as a result of their employment. NOTHING. And the biggest debates I have had were over a free cup of coffee. Policy is clear, NOTHING, yet many emergency services workers (police, fire, paramedics) are often offered a free cup of coffee. Technically, we are not allowed to accept it, so what should they do?

I always told them to leave the money on the table. If the waitress chooses to pay the bill or take it as a tip, that is their call. We must do what is right. I taught the people on my course that if, in the worst case, the server wouldn't take your money for the coffee, then pay for the person behind you. How can they complain when we paid for their coffee instead? In all the years I have taught ethics, coffee is still the most debated issue.

During my Ethics Training sessions, many members would ask me the "What if" questions. What if I can't pay for a guy's overtime, so I let them claim a meal that they didn't eat? *Well, I would tell them, that is fraud, not only on the part of the employee putting in the claim, but also on the part of the supervisor for certifying that it was a legitimate claim and signing to that effect.*

What if I am required to be on standby, but my daughter is skating out of town—can I get the government discount at the hotel? *No.*

It became my job to tell employees that they couldn't use the photocopier at work to photocopy stuff for their kids' homework or take batteries home for their kids' Christmas presents. At one detachment, they went through hundreds of nine-volt batteries, and when they checked the office inventory, there was NOT one thing that required a nine-volt battery.

In the end, ethics became part of the Supervisors course and the Source/ Agent Handlers course. Once again, this resulted in a lot of travel, this time to Alberta, Saskatchewan, New Brunswick and Quebec. Since I was the only bilingual member who taught Ethics Training, I was asked to travel to Quebec to teach in French on every course they had. I could feel myself starting to go downhill again.

After years of enduring sexual harassment, sexual assaults, being put at risk on the job, and all the travelling, I found myself being angry. I was angry all the time. I was having a very difficult time dealing with my anger. I was having outbursts at home and work, but mostly at home and I was drinking daily. At one point, the RCMP doctor commented on my drinking and told me I needed to cut back to one drink a day. Three years later, I saw the same RCMP doctor and he gave me the same advice, but by that point my drinking had become a lot worse. It became harder and harder to deal with my anger and the anxiety of going into work.

Chapter Thirty-Nine

🍁

IN JUNE 2010, I WAS assigned to work the G20 in Toronto, working at the Metro Toronto Convention Centre. My assignment was to take the lead on the media escort portion of the security detail. I was responsible for arranging escorts of the media to the rooms where the heads of state would meet. At times, that would require escorting media personnel to various locations within the Convention Centre or Intercontinental and Royal York Hotels in order to preserve security integrity.

Ultimately, I was in charge of escorting the media to the rooms where world leaders were holding a press conference.

Near the end of the conference, there is a photo op where all of the world leaders enter a conference room to have their pictures taken together. It's the highest level of risk as they're all confined to one room, and it was up to me to keep the media outside the room until everything was set. As soon as I opened the door, the media starting pushing and shoving to get into the room. Placing my body in the doorway, I yelled that if they didn't enter the door in an orderly fashion, I would close it and no pictures would be taken. They agreed and only then did I allow them to enter the room.

At one point, I heard loud cheering and stopped to see what was happening. Young people from around the world who were in attendance at the World Youth Leadership Conference being held at the same time were cheering because Barack Obama had just walked into the room. He was the only world leader they cheered for. It was a great moment.

It was quite the opposite, though, during the riots at the G20 when we were trapped in the Convention Centre. Rioters were burning police cars and damaging properties in and around our location. As a result, we had to be taken by bus to and from work every day, adding an hour to each shift we worked.

BACK in London, the work environment was getting difficult for me at this time because there wasn't enough work to keep me occupied. Approaching my superior officers, I asked what could be done about this and was told to bring in my own activities like books or puzzles to keep myself busy. I started to do more teaching on Supervisors courses and Source Agent Development courses, but it just wasn't enough.

Eventually, I asked to be assigned back to a detachment, but there were no vacancies. I had way too much time on my hands to think. And that wasn't good for me. I started to slide. My depression got worse and I started drinking at night to help me fall asleep. Then I started drinking more and more.

During this dark period in my life, I often thought about how I was going to kill myself. I even googled how to commit suicide. I wanted the fastest way to die, but I didn't want to suffer. When I had my gun, I thought about shooting myself, but I didn't want anyone to find me that way. I even thought about places where I would commit suicide. I had one special place picked out, but it was so remote that no one would ever find me. I didn't want people wondering if I were alive or not. That would be cruel.

My brain was always going a million miles an hour. Dark thoughts, bad dreams, noise. I couldn't stop the noise inside my head. I had constant headaches. Every morning, I would wake up tired and feeling as if I'd been in a fight. And the mood swings! From angry to sad, back to angry, and everything in between. Never happy, however.

It was even hard to be around happy people because I'd forgotten what that felt like. Instead, I felt angry because they were happy and I was not. The people who care for me the most are the ones I pushed away the hardest. I wanted to be left alone, but I hated being alone.

I didn't want to leave the house in case I lost control, got angry, or said something in front of people that I would later regret. I'd done that too often and the people I love had to apologize for my actions too many times. I was a wreck!

But who could I tell? What would they think of me? I was an RCMP officer—a Canadian icon of strength and stability. I would be letting every-one down if I revealed how I really felt. So I struggled every day to see the positive. I painted on a smile at work, but it came off when I got home.

IN 2011, a major event in the RCMP had a profound effect on me person-ally. Catherine Galliford came forward with allegations of extensive sexual harassment and misconduct within the RCMP. After she came forward, the RCMP denied her accusations and sought to dismiss her from the force. But I knew what Catherine had gone through was true. It was similar to what had happened to me. I was glued to her story and so proud of her bravery for coming forward, but I also watched as the RCMP denied everything and made her look like a drunk with issues.

By this point, I decided that my own situation was bad enough and I finally reached out for help. I started seeing a psychologist that year, and during our first meeting, I cried for the entire hour. I could barely tell her my name. I was in a very bad place.

I went to see her every week, then biweekly and then once a month. Initially, I didn't tell her how much I was drinking or what I'd gone through as she had to submit reports to the RCMP and I didn't trust the RCMP anymore.

After a year, I was diagnosed with PTSD. I knew I'd probably had it for a long time. And this diagnosis came well before she even knew about the rape. It took me over three years to be able to share that with her. I was still embarrassed that I'd allowed that to happen and still blamed myself.

I ended up telling her everything, though, including the fact that I was suicidal at times. Christmas always seemed to be the worst. I would start to feel better, then something would trigger my emotions and I would be a wreck again. There were days that dying was the only solution I thought would work. I also finally told her how much I was drinking, and from the look on her face, I could tell she was shocked.

She came up with a plan to help reduce my drinking. I can't say that I followed her plan at first because I wasn't ready to stop drinking. I was hurting, and booze was the only thing at the time that helped me deal with the stress. Over time, however, I started to make headway in reducing my alcohol intake and received some coping skills to help me deal with what had happened to me throughout my career.

SLOWLY, I started to feel better and, being back home, I had the support and help I needed. As I started to feel better, I looked into teaching again. I'd given a lecture on ethics to the Police Foundations students at Fanshawe College, and the instructor asked me if I wanted to teach as part of the Police Foundations program. He told me I should apply to teach part-time since I was still working with the RCMP. So I filled out all the appropriate paperwork required for both the RCMP and Fanshawe College, and was hired to teach four hours a week.

The first semester was the best. Teaching law is really straightforward, and I was provided with the PowerPoint slides from the previous instructor.

I really enjoyed the students. The next semester, my hours doubled to eight per week and I was also asked to teach a different topic that didn't already have a lesson plan or slides. Over the summer, I tried to put something together, but the material seemed to be unsuitable. In the end, I did put a plan together, but I was uncomfortable with the topic and disappointed with the results.

Chapter Forty

🍁

MEANWHILE, THINGS WERE COMING TO a head in the RCMP. In March 2012, a group of women came forward to start a class action lawsuit against the RCMP. W5 on CTV had aired an episode about four female members who'd been sexually assaulted while working undercover with a male member. This was what almost happened to me in Barrie. I can't even tell you how guilty this made me feel. What if I had come forward at the time—would this have happened?

It took me a long time to understand that the RCMP just wasn't ready to hear this, let alone deal with the sexual harassment that had taken place. For years and years, we'd been told that changes were coming, that accountability was coming, but it never came. Now there was definitely a shift in public perception about behaviour in the RCMP, and perhaps now, they would have to be ready to hear it and deal with it.

AT this time, I took a month off for stress leave. I needed to get away from the stress at work, or else all of my recovery would be undone and I would crash. When I came back to work, I was assigned to another section. Fortunately for me, this section needed a lot of help since they had two new staff and the operation of the section was a mess. Together the three of us there worked hard and turned it around, and it became a high functioning section. This was very satisfying work for me.

At one point, the Commanding Officer asked to speak with me. I was afraid that I'd be forced to move back to my old section, but instead, another opportunity of a lifetime was to present itself. She told me the RCMP had an opportunity to send a member to the Ontario Police College to become an instructor. I'd been getting a lot of great feedback about my training, and word that I was teaching at Fanshawe had gotten back to the boss. She thought of me right away. Advising me to get a résumé ready, she told me to take it to the college.

The next day, when I dropped off my résumé, I was interviewed right then and there. After about forty-five minutes I was told, "Welcome to the Ontario Police College." What a day!

IN August 2013, I started working at the Ontario Police College in Aylmer, Ontario on what was to be a two-year contract. I was eligible to retire soon, I thought to myself that maybe I would retire when my teaching contract finished. It would be a great way to end my career!

When I arrived, though, to my surprise, there were no recruits. That was strange. Apparently, the college had an intake of recruits which lasted three months, then it had a month without recruits. This was the cycle. In Depot, recruits just kept coming and it ran for twelve months of the years training recruits. This would be an adjustment.

I used the time to find my way around the college and prepare for my classes, having been given a binder of the materials I was to teach. My topic was Federal Stats, which is basically the *Criminal Code*, and that included all the work I was familiar with such as fraud and drugs. It felt good to be teaching something in line with my knowledge and experience. The binder set out word-for-word what I was supposed to say, what questions I might get asked and suggested responses to those questions.

Initially, I thought that was great. Everything I needed right in front of me. But I'd never taught that way before. This might be harder than it looked.

The supervisor gave me and another new instructor a chance to practise one of the sessions. At the end of my presentation, my lesson plan indicated I should send the cadets out to gather information about the instructor. The instructors in the class said, "We don't do that anymore".

So I asked the supervisor, "Do I keep it in or take it out of the lesson plan?"

The supervisor said that it was to stay in. This would be my first experience where lesson plans were not always followed. The other issue with the lesson plans was that they were filled with spelling mistakes. It was embarrassing to put up on the PowerPoint presentation and have to apologize to the students for all the mistakes. Nevertheless, I carried on as instructed.

AS the start of the intake got closer, my excitement grew—I couldn't wait to start. When the first day arrived at last, I stood and looked out the window as hundreds of cars were pulling into the Police College. Then, going down to the main lobby, I watched the cadets checking in. They had formed in a long line which was slowly as they entering the lecture hall.

I walked in to see what was happening in there, and to my dismay, the cadets were handing over cheques. When I asked what was going on, one staff member informed me the cadets have to pay to attend the Police College. The cost was $7,000. That was so different from what I'd experienced as an RCMP officer. But this was just the beginning of a whole new learning experience for me.

Once the cadets had signed in, paid their fees and settled themselves, classes began. Each intake could train 240 cadets, at the most. The college couldn't take on any more than that due to legislation on the number of rolls of bullets each cadet must shoot before they leave. So during the first intake, I taught law to approximately 240 recruits from various police services throughout Ontario. Teaching at Fanshawe College has been good, but this was going to be great—I loved teaching!

INSTRUCTORS at Police College are seconded from various police services based on their particular experiences in traffic, investigations, etc. It was, however, difficult to find instructors with a training background, as many officers didn't want to live away from home for two years, which was the average length of a secondment. If an officer were seconded from Thunder Bay, for instance, they might only get home three or four times a year, and it was difficult to convince them to be away from home for such long periods of time.

Because of this, during my first intake, the Chief Instructor asked me if I would be interested in a full-time teaching position at the college.

Since I was nearing retirement from the RCMP, I told him that I'd be very interested. It might take a year or two to hire me, he admitted, but in the meantime, I could use my time there to gain experience to add to my résumé. I was over the moon!

I was the only female instructor on my section of ten instructors and, as usual, it wouldn't take long before this became a problem. One of the topics that I had to teach the recruits was sexual assault. Having been a victim myself, I wasn't sure if I could teach it without becoming emotional, and found myself getting very stressed and experiencing anxiety about teaching this material.

Approaching a co-worker, I confided to him that I'd been a victim of sexual assault and asked if he would teach this topic to my students instead. That way, I could also watch the way he taught it and use his examples in future lessons. I was greatly relieved when he agreed to do so, since this was turning out to be very challenging for me and was not getting any better.

Soon, I started to see that, like the RCMP, the Police College had its own set of issues. I tried to stay focused on my tasks and not get involved in them, but the longer I was there, the more difficult that became. Cuts to staff and other changes were coming that the staff didn't approve of, causing the work environment to become stressful. Male instructors attended the same off-campus bars as the recruits, resulting in complaints about inappropriate contact between themselves and female recruits. Some seconded instructors even bragged how they'd watch the women in their dorms getting dressed and undressed, since they didn't close the blinds.

There was also a distinct feeling of a two-tiered staff system, with the permanent instructors seeming neither to like nor trust the seconded instructors. Since there was always talking and hoping among the seconded instructors about getting a full-time job teaching at the college, I guess the permanent instructors felt threatened.

ONE of the most stressful days for the cadets was the day they got pepper sprayed. I told my students I would go with them to cheer them on, and when I arrived to watch the first group, it was great to see that each group had support assigned to help them. The blind leading the blind, literally.

First, the cadets were pepper sprayed, then they had to get into a fighting situation, call for backup and make an arrest, all while their eyes were burning from the spray. Once they'd completed their scenario, their support person would wrap their face in a towel and lead them to a chair to sit down where a sprayer full of water was available to help rinse their eyes.

From personal experience, I knew that air, not water, was the best cure for pepper spray, so I ran to the cafeteria to get some lunch trays. Returning with about twenty of them, I told the support people to fan the faces of the cadets while they held their eyes open. I knew for a fact that this was the best thing to relieve the pain. Then I walked from one person to the next and talked to them in a slow, calm voice to get them to concentrate on me instead of the pain. That night, the cadets told their fellow cadets that what I'd done had worked better than the water, and I was asked by the other cadets to attend their pepper spray classes and help them too. I attended every single session—how could I say no?

As I took more trays, though, the kitchen staff became upset with me since they didn't want their trays to get contaminated. So one of the directors arranged to get twenty trays permanently assigned to the pepper spray session.

There were two occasions, after the college nurse had already left the pepper spray session, that a cadet suffered a severe reaction to the spray. In one case, the cadet collapsed on the floor, couldn't catch his breath and was fading in and out of consciousness. Having bent down on the floor beside him, I asked the other cadets to get me a towel to place under his head. Of course, all the towels were contaminated with pepper spray. So instead, I lay down and placed my arm under his head to keep it from hitting the floor while I held him with my other arm and kept talking to him, telling him he was going to be okay. He was taken away by ambulance. On the second occasion, the cadet hyper ventilated but recovered and did not required any medical treatment.

The following day, I was called into the Chief Director's office and told that I shouldn't have done what I did. I pleaded my case, that I was just trying to help the cadet remain calm, but was told the next time to wait for help to arrive. Then I started getting teased by a few instructors, asking me to hold them and hug them. To me, we should be able to be caring and show compassion to someone in distress, let alone a cadet having a serious reaction to pepper spray. I just didn't understand why that was an issue.

I was asked not to attend any further sessions. I'd been thanked by so many cadets for being there and offering my support that I couldn't believe I'd done the wrong thing. Although I didn't agreed with what was asked of me, I stayed away.

I also assisted at night acting as a "drunk" while cadets learned how to handle vehicle stops. In one scenario, I was the passenger in the back seat as my brother, who was sober, came to pick me up. I had an open beer in my hand. The cadets were to seize the beer, write me a ticket and release us to go home.

The cadets removed the beer from my hand and placed it on top on the vehicle, but then I opened a second bottle of beer to show them that they should always check to see if there are any more. If the cadet left the beer on the roof of the car, I would reach out, grab it and start drinking from it again. This was so much fun!

We laughed about that during the briefing, and I was asked to participate in more scenarios. What an excellent learning opportunity. I was having the best time of my life sharing my policing experiences with these cadets.

Chapter Forty-One

✿

IN BETWEEN THE FIRST AND second intakes, I had a month with no teaching and nothing else to do, so I decided that I'd take the lesson plans and PowerPoint presentations and correct the mistakes. It took me about three weeks to get all the errors corrected. Lastly, I printed off the materials and saved the new corrected material to be uploaded on the Police College's server. But when I approached the Chief Instructor and provided him with a copy of the new material, letting him know that I'd corrected the errors in the teaching materials, he brushed me off, saying that was not my job. He took the material and stuffed it in the secure recycle bin.

I was shaken. Back in my office, I thought there must have been a miscommunication, so I decided to return and try to explain what I'd done. Taking the old material and placing the new material beside it, I went through the presentation page by page. Finally, he got it. I figure he'd thought I was trying to rewrite the material when all I'd done was correct the grammar and spelling.

Once he understood what I had accomplished, he asked the secretary for the key to the recycle bin, unlocked it and retrieved my original material. But still, he didn't seem to be too impressed with me. I just wanted our teaching materials to look professional and felt that the Ontario Police College should set a high standard of excellence. For some reason that I couldn't understand, the relationship between the Chief Instructor and myself was never very good after this incident.

DURING the second intake, two addition female officers joined our team of instructors. One had previously taught at the Police College years ago in the area of Driver Training, but had no idea what to do in Federal Stats. Since I knew what it felt like to be on my own learning the materials, I took her under my wing and taught her what I could. She had also never used a computer or PowerPoint, so I gradually taught her how to use these too. She would watch me as I taught my classes and I'd sit in the back of her classes in case she needed help. On many occasions, she would ask me to help clarify a point or answer a question that she could not, and I was happy to do so. She also gave me a copy of the letter she'd written to our supervisor, praising me for the help I had given her, but the supervisor never acknowledged the letter.

Although this was a new supervisor, I wondered if he'd been warned about me by the previous one. From day one, he was cold and distant with me, and never had a nice thing to say to me. I tried to win him over, but he just didn't seem to like me.

One day, he called me in and told me I could no longer help cadets who attended my office to ask a question or who needed a point clarified. During the first intake, we were encouraged to help the cadets. What had changed?

Within a week or two, I was called into his office again and told that I was being moved to Driver Training during the next intake. I felt like I was being punished for trying to help cadets learn the law. I was confused and disappointed, but I tried to stay positive and look at it as a new learning opportunity.

Sadly, things would only get worse.

Near the end of the second intake, I warned the female cadets to close their blinds so that no one could see them changing. I also told them that, as women, they would have to work extra hard and would not be viewed as equal to their male coworkers. One of the cadets agreed with these comments, mentioning she'd been an auxiliary member with the OPP and knew first-hand that what I was saying was true.

The next day, before class, another female instructor told me she'd reported me to the Chief Instructor because she'd taken issue with what I'd said to those cadets, and let me know that the he wanted to talk to me. I wish I'd realized that I was too emotional at this point to handle this type of confrontation, but I didn't understand how fragile I was. This situation led to another meltdown on my part.

I was told I wouldn't be allowed to finish teaching during this intake— other instructors were assigned to teach my classes—but could remain at the college. At first, I wasn't even allowed to sit in the back of the class-room. And when my students kept asking me why I wasn't teaching them anymore, especially with final exams being so close at hand, I told them it hadn't been my decision.

AT the start of the third intake, we were advised that a guest speaker would be coming to talk to us about adult learning and self-learning. The RCMP had already incorporated those into their training, but the Police College hadn't. So when the speaker asked a question about adult learning, I raised my hand to answer, and after I'd finished, my supervisor from the second intake lit into me right on the spot. "Who do you think you are?" he shouted.

The rest of his remarks are a blank as I was dumbfounded that he was berating me in front of all of the instructors and the guest speaker. One of the full- time instructors approached me later that day, stating she was putting in a complaint against him for the way he'd treated me. I thanked her for her support.

Within a couple of days the Chief Instructor I'd worked for in Federal Stats approached me and told me I was no longer allowed to teach Cross Fit to the recruits. I was in disbelief. Now what? When I approached the Fitness Instructors to advise them that I wouldn't be teaching Cross Fit anymore, they asked me, "Why not?" I told them to ask the Chief Instructor.

Things only continued to go downhill from there.

During Driver Training, one of the cadets became frustrated to the point of tears. While talking to her, I happened to put my hand on her shoulder to reassure her that the skills would come with practice. The next day, I was called in by the head of Driver Training and told that by no means was I ever to touch a cadet. He made it sound like I'd done something grossly inappropriate.

In the end, though, I was only able to work for three weeks in Driver Training before I injured my rotator cuff while demonstrating driving skills. I'd need surgery prior to continuing this type of training. I knew that by taking medical leave, my chances of getting a full-time job at the Police College were over, but I couldn't take the stress anymore, let alone the pain that was added to it from my injury. I was done.

During the long weekend in May, I packed up all my stuff and left. My feedback from the first two intakes had been amazing. I was rated the best instructor at the Ontario Police College for two intakes. Then it all went south. The dream of teaching was over.

LATER that year, I had rotator cuff surgery to repair a torn ligament, which prevented me from maintaining my personal fitness. I was off on sick leave for the next two years, and that is when the PTSD hit me hardest. I was exhausted. I've never been so tired in all my life. All I wanted to do was sleep. I was sleeping almost twelve to fourteen hours a day if not longer.

I continued to get the help I needed to deal with my PTSD, and during this time, I came to realize that I could never return to work for the RCMP. I waited for the RCMP's health services to recommend a medical discharge. Disappointingly, they never did, so I contacted the Medical Discharge Coordinator myself and put the medical discharge process into motion.

The Aftermath

🍁

IN 2016, THE CLASS ACTION lawsuit was certified and I was able to submit a claim for the sexual assault and harassment I had endured in my career in the RCMP. I debated long and hard about submitting a claim—I did not want to relive the trauma and pain I'd endured. I spoke to my psychologist at length as to whether or not I should submit a claim.

I decided to go forward with it, not just for myself, but for others, too, as I felt I had to do what I could to prevent what had happened to me from happening to future woman in policing. I also felt strongly that this needed to be done for all women in a male-dominated workplace so that people like my nieces would be protected when they entered the workforce. It was too late to change things for me, but I could help change things for them.

AS I prepared my submission for the lawsuit, I had to constantly relive the trauma of the sexual assault and the harassment that I endured. Sadly, as I had feared it would, my PTSD was triggered by those memories and I had trouble coping with them once again. After two years of sobriety, I began drinking again to numb the feelings.

During the process of writing up my claim, whenever it became too overwhelming, I would take a couple of weeks off from it. Then, when I felt better, I'd start writing again. And so it went until I finally hit the "SEND" button on my claim, and then promptly began to worry about where it would all lead.

My medical discharge was granted and I left the RCMP on January 16, 2017 after thirty years of service. There was no way I could have predicted that, thirty years earlier in New Brunswick, it would end this way, with me in this condition.

I joined a few online support groups of RCMP members who also had PTSD. The group setting was very supportive and a great place to be. I couldn't believe there were people who were going through the same things as I was. When someone posted how they were feeling, it was almost as if they were reading my thoughts and feelings. I wasn't crazy after all.

It took me over a year before I trusted the site enough to tell people my real name. Even my Facebook account was in my dog's name. I was in a place where I didn't trust anyone in or associated with the RCMP. Recently, one of those members committed suicide, and I was devastated and suffered a major setback in my healing process, requiring a great deal of extra counselling. Eventually, I arrived at a better place and made my peace with her loss, but those unexpected stumbling blocks always seem to be just around the corner.

RETIREMENT is wonderful, but not without some scars from the job. After a lifetime of policing, it's hard to stop looking around for criminal activity. Hard to let down your guard. Hard to trust people. Hard to forget the things you have seen.

In hindsight, I honestly believe my greatest asset became my ultimate downfall. I cared too much. I wanted to make a difference so badly! When I'd realized that the RCMP was not the perfect institution I had imagined it would be, I was determined to improve it in any way I could. I'd refused to become cynical and accept the flaws.

I still do a lot of reflecting and wondering about what I could have done differently. Which decisions were the right ones and which were the wrong ones? I know, deep down in my heart, that the abuse was not my fault at all, but the fault of the men and of the institution that allowed it, yet I continue to wonder how I might have stopped it.

MONTHS later, I received an email from a lawyer from the Merlo Davidson Group stating that my submission was assigned and was being reviewed. Within a month of that email, I was contacted again to set up a date for an interview. Only claims at the higher levels would receive an interview.

My friend Jennifer, also a claimant, offered to go with me to the interview. I felt as if I should bring her as she'd helped me along the way during this process and this was my way of helping her too. She'd get to see the process first hand and that would help her when it came her turn to be interviewed.

Once the date for the interview was set, I'd sort of shut down. Jennifer took care of all the travel arrangements to get to Toronto and to the office where the interview would be held.

SO there I sat, and the judge had just asked me why I had wanted to become an RCMP officer. I told him much of the story I have written here in these pages.

During the conversation, he encouraged me to talk and only asked a couple of questions. One question was why I'd not gone on stress leave after I had been sexually assaulted. When talking about the sexual assault, I had cried, and to my surprise, there were tears in the judge's eyes too. I told him that if I had gone on stress leave then, I didn't think I'd ever have come back to work. Stress leave was looked at very poorly by other members, who think you are faking an illness, referring to it as "sad leave" or "mad leave".

I didn't bring any written notes with me to the interview. Everything was in my head and I didn't need it in front of me to remember. Then, finally, I took out the one thing I *had* prepared—a picture of my three nieces—and placed it in front of the judge, telling him that they were the reason I was sitting in front of him. I told him who they were and that it was important to me to make the workforce a safer place for them, a safer place than it had been for me. I also told him that I would do everything within my power to make sure that none of them ever entered law enforcement, as I didn't have any faith that this process would lead to positive changes to the RCMP.

The judge tried to assure me that he had the ear of the prime minister. But I reminded him that the process would take another three years to complete and that the prime minister might not be in that position by the time he made his recommendations. It would take significant changes in legislation as well as funding to make some real improvements in the RCMP. Without serious consequences for their actions, members would not change. They needed to understand that their jobs, benefits and pensions were at risk when they engaged in inappropriate behavior.

I shared with the judge how I thought the RCMP was doing the same thing the Catholic Church has been accused of doing—members who needed to be disciplined were instead promoted or transferred to other detachments, where new victims awaited them. Thanking him for listening to my story, I wished him the best of luck with his project.

After the interview, I was exhausted and felt that way for several days. Of course, I replayed the interview over and over again in my mind. It felt so good to tell someone at last what had happened to me—someone whom I could place my trust in, someone who could potentially help to make the changes needed. He had done it without judgment, without doubts, without questioning my integrity.

It was a relief to just say the words out loud. I'd been saying them to myself long enough.

IN spite of what happened to me, I want you to know that I've worked with some of the best men and women in law enforcement. I am proud of my service, and my chest still puffs out when I wear the Red Serge. I worked very hard to earn the chance to wear it and even harder to keep it. I haven't given up on the belief that the RCMP can only get better, but the changes that need to be made are coming too late for a whole generation of female officers who have experienced the types of abuse and discrimination that I did, despite of our very best intentions.

When I first sat in that police cruiser in New Brunswick many years ago, I was young and naïve and couldn't imagine any career more wonderful than being a Mountie. I'm not that person anymore, and I don't always like the person I have become.

It seems that I'll continue to ride the PTSD rollercoaster, but hope there will be more good days than bad. The optimist still living deep inside of me looks forward to hearing that all the efforts of the women who are now coming forward are leading to the changes that need to be made to this proud Canadian institution.

Printed in Canada